TIME SEARCH

History through Evidence ♦ Julia Cigman & John Halsall **BOOK THREE**

Oxford University Press 1988

The publishers would like to thank the following for permission to reproduce copyright material:

p.6 Ann Ronan Picture Library; p.7 top left and bottom right British Museum, centre Michael Holford, top right E T Archive, bottom left Robert Harding; pp. 8,9,10,11,12 and 13 Author's Collection; p.15 left Robert Harding, right Scottish Tourist Board; p.16 Mrs John Loudon; p.17 top N Yorks County Libraries, bottom City Museums and Art Gallery, Birmingham; p.19 Barnaby's; p.20 J Allan Cash; p.21 Robert Harding; p.23 J Allan Cash; p.24 Editions d'Art Albert Skira S A; p.25 top left Michael Holford, centre right Robert Harding, bottom right John Brennan; p.26 background *Illustrated London News*, top right Air Canada; p.28 The Post Office; p.29 top centre John Brennan, others The Post Office; p.33 Sally & Richard Greenhill; p.34 top left and right Robert Harding, top centre Biofotos, bottom Michael Holford; p.35 top left Michael Holford, top centre Format, top right J Allan Cash, bottom left Susan Griggs, bottom right Barnaby's; p.42 top Aerofilms; p.43 left and bottom John Brennan, centre left Marion & Tony Morrison; p.44 centre Mansell Collection, left Woodmansterne; p.46 Woodmansterne; pp.49 and 50 E T Archive; p.52 Michael Holford; p.53 top left E T Archive, centre left Mary Evans Picture Library, bottom left Sally & Richard Greenhill; p.54 top left Robert Harding, centre Susan Griggs, bottom left John Brennan; p.55 top right Oxford University Press, centre Ann Ronan Picture Library, bottom left *Punch*; p.56 The Boots Company PLC; p.57 top left Sally & Richard Greenhill, top right E T Archive, bottom left Mary Evans Picture Library, bottom right Robert Harding; p.59 top The Bridgeman Art Library, centre left Guy's Hospital, centre Ken Moreman, right Mansell Collection; p.60 Ann Ronan Picture Library, top right The Science Museum, centre right Robert Harding, centre left The Wellcome Institute, bottom Camilla Jessel; p.62 Richardson-Vicks Ltd; p.63 left RSPCA, right John Brennan; p.64 centre left E T Archive, bottom left Michael Holford; p.65 top left E T Archive, top right Dickens House Museum, bottom left Mary Evans Picture Library, bottom right London Weekend Television; p.66 BBC Enterprises Ltd; p.67 Rex Features; p.71 E T Archive; p.73 Nobby Clark; pp. 74 and 75 British Museum; p.76 Robert Harding; p.77 Simon Warner; p.80 The Ashmolean Museum; p.81 centre right Oxford Scientific Films, bottom John Brennan; p.82 Colorsport; p.83 top AMCA, bottom Fine Art Photographers; p.86 the Bridgeman Art Library; p.87 E T Archive; p.88 BBC Hulton Picture Library; p.89 The Mansell Collection; p.90 top left John Brennan, top centre Museum of London, centre and centre right Michael Holford, right Mary Evans Picture Library; p.91 The Fotomas Index; p.92 bottom left Oxford County Libraries, bottom right John Brennan; p.93 top Oxford County Libraries, right Waltham Forest Libraries; p.94 top left and bottom National Film Archive, centre right Museum of London; p. 95 right Imperial War Museum, bottom left and centre Susan Griggs, bottom right National Film Archive.

The illustrations are by Mark Bergin, John Brennan, Nick Harris, Nick Hawken, Christa Hook, Richard Hook, Andrew Howat, Ed McLachlan, Christine Molan, Tony Morris, Maggie Silver, Malcolm Stokes, Michael Whittlesea and Melvyn Wright.

Oxford University Press, Walton Street, Oxford OX2 6DP

Oxford New York Toronto
Delhi Bombay Calcutta Madras Karachi
Petaling Jaya Singapore Hong Kong Tokyo
Nairobi Dar es Salaam Cape Town
Melbourne Auckland

and associated companies in
Berlin, Ibadan

Oxford is a trade mark of Oxford University Press

© Julia Cigman & John Halsall 1988
ISBN 0 19 917098 3

Set by Tradespools Ltd, Frome
Printed in Hong Kong

CONTENTS

EVIDENCE

LOOKING AT OBJECTS
- A Bridge from the Past — 4
- Scientific Jigsaw Puzzles — 6

LOOKING AT PICTURES
- Cow Keepers and Bell Hangers — 8
- The Nita Suta — 10
- Ironmonger to the King — 12

TALKING TO PEOPLE
- Kings on the Run — 14
- Singers on the Roof — 16
- 1 *Finding time* — 18

LOOKING AT BUILDINGS
- Stud and Mud — 20
- A Long Walk — 22
- How Big is a Brick? — 24

LOOKING AT WRITING
- The Royal Mail — 26
- Second Class Post — 28
- The History of ... You? — 30
- 2 *Finding time* — 32

CHANGES

SETTLING NEW LANDS
- Explorers and Settlers — 34
- Discovering America — 36
- Settlers – the Pilgrim Fathers — 38
- Making a New Home — 40
- 3 *Finding time* — 42

FINDING OUT ABOUT THE WORLD
- The Medieval Picture of the World — 44
- Scribes and Storytellers — 46
- Spreading the Word — 48
- The Shrinking World — 50
- 4 *Finding time* — 52

MEDICINE AND HEALTH
- Clean and Healthy — 54
- Going to the Doctor — 56
- New Discoveries — 58
- Going to Hospital — 60
- 5 *Finding time* — 62

PROJECT

ENTERTAINMENT
- Playtime — 64
- 'Once upon a Time ...' — 66
- A Pilgrim Storyteller — 68
- On the Road — 70
- In the Market Square — 72
- The Wooden 'O' — 74
- A Story and a Play — 76
- A Relaxing Interval — 78
- The Falcon and the White Hart — 80
- Practising for War — 82
- Holding a Tournament — 84
- The Sealed Knot — 86
- Holy Days – Fasting and Football — 88
- Remember, Remember, the fifth of November ... — 90
- All the Fun of the Fair — 92
- Talking Pictures — 94
- Index — 96

EVIDENCE

LOOKING AT OBJECTS

A Bridge from the Past

One way in which we learn about people who lived long ago is by digging up the things that they left behind. They threw things away when they were broken. They lost a lot of things. Sometimes, they buried things to hide them from robbers and were killed before they could dig them up again. Very often, a man's things would be buried with him when he died.

When things are dug up, they are dirty and sometimes broken. Before the archaeologist can learn anything from them, he or she has to know *what* they are and *how old* they are. Most important of all, the archaeologist has to know where they were found and the order in which they were dug up.

Let us pretend that we are archaeologists and that we have dug up the things you see on this page. Before you read on, have a good look at them. See if you can tell what they are.

The first thing to be dug up was found quite near the surface. It is part of a violin. It is the bridge that holds up the strings. It seems to be perfect.

A bit further down in the ground was the wooden broom head. The handle is missing, but you can see the holes where the bristles used to be.

Underneath that was the sound box from an old-fashioned record player which was called a gramophone. The rest of the gramophone was not there. The sound box held the needle that rested on the gramophone record when it played.

Last of all, the deepest, was the brass top of an electric lamp. There were nine of these lying among a lot of broken glass.

Now that we have found out what they are, we have to try and date them.

The design of a violin has not changed very much since 1600, so that bridge might have been thrown away at any time during the last 400 years.

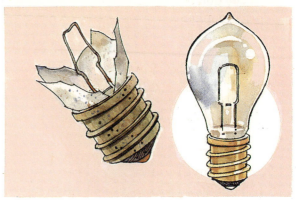

LOOKING AT OBJECTS

EVIDENCE

Brushes like the one here came into use about 1890, and they are still being made, so this broom must have been thrown away during the last 100 years.

The gramophone was invented in 1878, but a sound box like this would not have been made until about 1910. Electrical recording began about 1930, so this sound box must have been made during the twenty years between 1910 and 1930.

Electric lamps like this were first made about 1913, but we in England have only recently had lamps with screw fittings, so these lamps must be either very new or foreign.

Now that we have rough dates for all the things, let us look at them a little more closely. The gramophone sound box has the words 'Lion Phonographe' stamped round the edge. 'Phonograph' is the American word for gramophone, but 'Phonographe' with an 'e' on the end is French. Perhaps this gramophone belonged to a rich man who went over to France to buy it.

When we measure the broom head we find that it is almost exactly 350 mm (35 cm). Brushes made in England at that time would have been measured in inches. It looks as if this broom might have come from France too.

A rich English person might go to France to buy a gramophone, but he or she would not go all that way to buy a broom.

And what about all those electric lamps that seem to have been thrown away at the same time?

Well, as it happens, electric lamps in France have always had screw fittings.

Suppose that somebody lived in France and suddenly had to come to live in England. They would bring all their furniture and other things with them. When they got to England they would find that their French electric lamps were no good and had to be thrown away.

Quite a lot of English people lived and worked in France. In 1914, a war broke out and the invading German army nearly captured Paris. Many English people left their homes in France and came back to England. Perhaps we have found the home of a family that did just that.

We know that the electric lamps were the first things to be thrown away because they were at the bottom of the heap, and this must have happened after 1913. The broom soon wore out and the head was thrown away but the handle was kept.

Some time later, the sound box of the gramophone broke and the family had to buy a new one.

The violin was used by a boy or a girl. When the child grew up, he or she needed a slightly higher bridge, and the old one found its way on to the rubbish heap.

5

EVIDENCE

LOOKING AT OBJECTS
Scientific Jigsaw Puzzles

Men and women first walked the earth nearly two million years ago. In one way they were exactly like us. They had to eat.

Through the ages, people have always left behind the weapons and tools they used for hunting and growing food. Most important of all, they learned how to make pots of baked clay for storing and cooking their food.

Perhaps we can guess how people first had the idea of making pots. Suppose they had been out hunting in very wet weather. When they got back they made a fire on the wet ground to warm themselves and cook their food. The next day, they might notice that some of the wet clay under the fire had baked hard. When rain fell again, hollows in the baked clay would fill with water, just like little cups.

Things made of wood and bone soon rot away, but once clay has been baked in a fire there is no reason why it should not last for ever. When archaeologists are digging, they nearly always find hundreds of pieces of broken pottery. If they can put a pot back together again they can often tell how old it is and who made it. But it is like trying to do a jigsaw puzzle when you have the pieces of a hundred jigsaws all mixed up together.

The pictures show different ways pots have been made, from the first pots made about 10,000 years ago to the invention of the potter's wheel.

1. At first, pots were just modelled from solid lumps of clay.

2. Later, pots were formed by beating out the clay over a round stone.

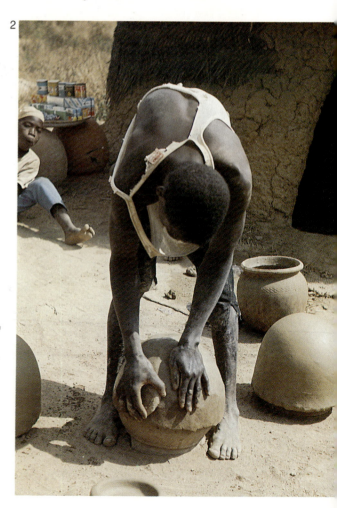

6

LOOKING AT OBJECTS

EVIDENCE

3. Here you can see a pot that has been built up from rings of clay.

4. By building up the pot from a coil of clay it was easier to control the shape.
5. If you had a good pot, you could make another one quite quickly by building the coils over it.

6. Pots are still made today on wheels like this one.
   Of course, once the pot has been shaped it has to be heated for several hours in a hot oven or kiln.
   One way to tell the age of a pot is by looking at *the things found with it*. The following pictures show pots that were found with other objects which helped to date them correctly.

7. This pot was found with a stone axe, and it must have been made in the Stone Age about 6,000 years ago.
8. This pot was found with a bronze spear-head and some bronze brooches. It cannot be more than 4,000 years old, because before then people did not know how to make things with bronze.

9. This pot was found with a broken iron sword blade, so it must have been made in the Iron Age and cannot be more than 2,500 years old.

10. This pot was found *above* some Roman paving stones and it must have been made in Saxon times about 1,200 years ago.
    Are you good at jigsaws? If you are, you might like to become an archaeologist.

7

EVIDENCE

LOOKING AT PICTURES

Cow Keepers and Bell Hangers

What was it like to live 10,000 years ago?

Archaeologists try to answer that question by digging in the ground. They have found things left behind by people who lived long ago.

What was it like to live 100 years ago?

You can find out by 'digging' into old magazines and newspapers and looking at the advertisements. We can learn a lot about how things have changed.

Here are just a few advertisements from a hundred years ago.

In those days, there were no cars and the horse was very important. Can you imagine going to the seaside for the day in a waggonette like the ones above?

It was not easy to make blocks for the printing of pictures, but the newspaper office always kept a few blocks that could be used by advertisers.

If you advertised your livery stable, you could ask for 'a suitable picture' to be put into your advertisement.

As you see, Mr Haydon got the same picture as Mr. Wills.

Of course, if there were a lot of horses there had to be a lot of people selling hay for fodder, and straw for bedding.

Most houses burned coal in open fireplaces for heating, and in huge iron ovens for cooking. But they did not need so much coal during the hot summer months.

Mr Collings sold hay and straw as well as coal so that he could keep busy all the year round.

Mr. Searle, the builder, could make coffins as well. He kept carriages and horses which could be hired out for funerals.

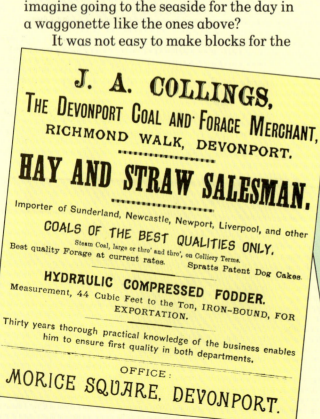

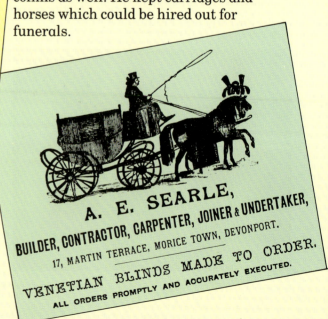

LOOKING AT PICTURES — EVIDENCE

Nowadays, most things are made in large numbers in huge factories and sent all over the world.

A hundred years ago nearly everything you needed could be made by somebody in the town where you lived.

If you went to see Mr. Colwill (opposite the Royal Hotel) he would show you no fewer than 38 different styles of hats and caps. He would take your measurements and make any style especially for you.

Look at all the things Mr. Wyatt could make at the Mutley Ironmongery Warehouse. He did not just *sell* gas fires and cooking stoves – he *made* them. He made knives, forks and spoons, too. And can you imagine going to an ironmonger for a pair of spectacles?

Why do you suppose Mr. Wyatt thought it a good idea to advertise petroleum? And what on earth is Colza Oil?

Bottles of milk appear mysteriously on your doorstep every morning, but you don't always see your milkman every day.

If you go round to the dairy very early in the morning you might find a huge tanker bringing the milk. There would be a noisy machine filling the bottles and putting on the tops. You would certainly not see a cow.

Mr. Maddock would bring milk round to your house three or four times a day if you asked him. The milk would always be fresh from the cow.

A hundred years ago, Queen Victoria was on the throne of England and head of the British Empire. She was the Empress of India and Queen of Canada, Australia, New Zealand, most of Africa, hundreds of islands in the Atlantic, Pacific and Indian Oceans, and many other countries as well.

If you were a soldier in the British army, you might have to go and serve in any part of the Empire.

Every army officer had to have horses, so he had to have saddles and harnesses. He also had a set of equipment for looking after the horses.

You could order everything you needed from Mr. Randle. He would send it to you in any part of the world.

One thing is missing from all these advertisements. It is something you will find in every advertisement that appears in newspapers today. Have a good look and see if you can guess what it is.

It was invented in America in 1876, and in 1880 a few people had it in England. The first chance the public had to make use of it was in Swansea in 1881.

In 1911, the Post Office took it over everywhere except in Hull, and by 1912 there were about 700,000 of them in the country.

Because of the great war between 1914 and 1918 the numbers did not grow very quickly until 1920. Today, there are more than ten million of them in Britain.

Yes, it's the telephone.

Today you can sit in your room and dial a number in Australia. A hundred years ago you could not even telephone the milkman round the corner!

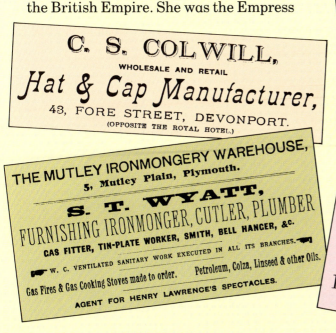

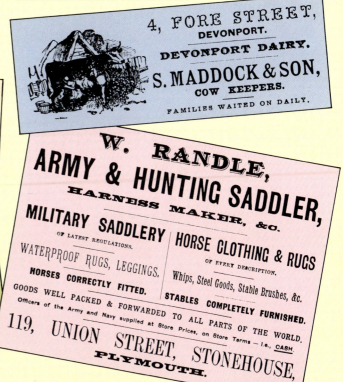

EVIDENCE

LOOKING AT PICTURES
The Nita Suta

Perhaps the most famous shop in the world is Harrod's of London. They claim that they can supply anything 'from a pin to an elephant'.

Every year they produce a catalogue to show the full range of goods that they have in stock. On these pages you can see some of the things they were selling in 1895.

Nobody knew how to print photographs in 1895, so every item had to be drawn by an artist.

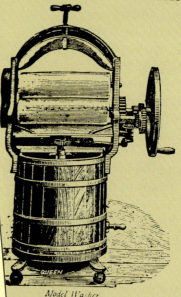

LOOKING AT PICTURES EVIDENCE

Customers all over the world could see the goods without having to come to the shop. They ordered goods by post. They still do.

Harrod's customers were usually quite rich, and they liked to keep up to date with all the latest things. They must have been quite excited to see these new washing machines.

The Vowel machine was filled with water, soap and dirty clothes, and the lid was screwed down tight to stop the water from spilling. When the handle was turned, the whole tank turned over and over and churned up the clothes in the water until they were clean.

The Model washer churned up the clothes in an open tub. When the clothes were clean, they could be lifted straight out of the tub. The water was then squeezed out of them between the big wooden rollers.

The dearer of the two machines cost £4. 5s (£4.25). Perhaps you think that it was very cheap. But in 1895 a working man, such as a bricklayer, clerk or shop assistant, would earn only about £2.50 a week. And if a woman worked, she earned even less. So the machine cost nearly two weeks' wages in those days. How much are washing machines now?

It must have been hard work turning those handles, but the people who bought these machines would be quite rich and they would have servants to do the hard work.

When the water had been squeezed out of the clothes, they could be hung on the Barnes Patent Clothes Dryer. There must be quite a few houses in Britain that still have dryers like this. Perhaps you know somebody who has one. How do you dry your clothes?

In 1895, a few people already had electric lighting in their houses. A lot more had gas lighting, but most houses would be lit by candles or oil lamps. Even if you had gas lighting you would use oil lamps as well. Oil was cheaper than gas, and an oil lamp could be carried from room to room. Can you think of any problems you might have with oil and gas lighting?

Oil lamps from the Harrod's catalogue

Would you have liked a 'Nita Suta'? You can see that the child without one is getting cold in bed, while the other child is sleeping snug and warm with a happy smile.

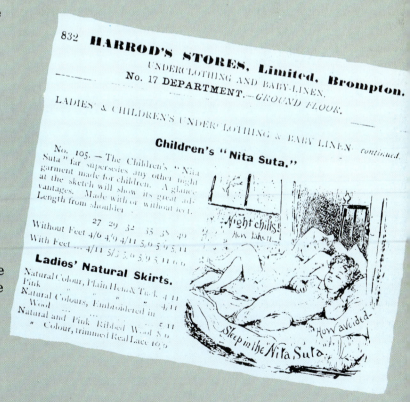

LOOKING AT PICTURES
Ironmonger to the King

The advertisements shown here are from the year 1915. Perhaps you think that things had not changed very much since the advertisements of 1888 that we saw on pages 8 and 9.

In 1915, England was at war with Germany and many men had joined the army or the navy. There was no air force then. We had some fighting aircraft, but all the pilots were in the army.

A great many people were still using horses for travelling about the country, and Mr. Dickson was still running a Posting House where you could change your horse if you were on a long journey.

If you had to move to a new house, White & Company would move your furniture for you with their steam engine. Steam engines like this are still in use. You might still see one at a circus.

Mr. White must have spent quite a lot of money buying that steam engine. Perhaps he wished that he had waited a bit longer, because you see that other furniture removers, like John Walton & Company, already had motor vans.

Look at all the things John Walton & Co have for sale. Can you imagine buying a new hat, a carpet, some nails and a packet of tea all in the same shop while you were making arrangements for your furniture to be removed?

Mr. J. J. Bone sells all sorts of things, but he thinks people will be more interested in his baths than anything else. He has decided to put a bath in his advertisement. Is it like your bath?

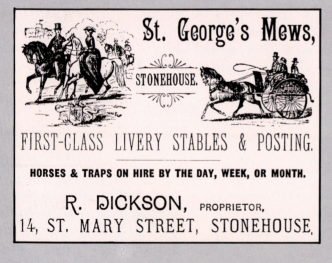

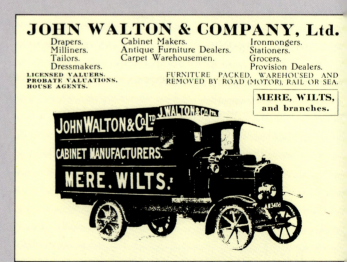

LOOKING AT PICTURES — EVIDENCE

In 1915, not many houses had baths with taps and running water. If you took a bath at all it would be in a bath like the Oxford Hip Bath. Somebody would have to carry the water to fill it. Worst of all, somebody would have to empty it afterwards.

Can you imagine why anyone would want to buy a bath just to wash their legs?

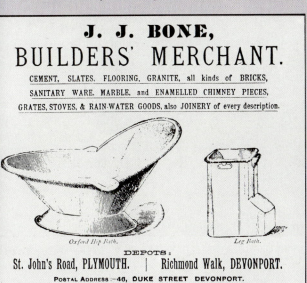

Mr. J. W. Savage has been in business as a stationer for 36 years, but now he wants to tell you about a wonderful new invention – rubber stamps.

Mr. Savage is a very smart man, and a very lucky one. He has one of those new talking instruments called telephones.

During the war, very few new telephone lines were laid. As you see, even the newspaper office of the Hants and Berks Gazette could not get a telephone, and they had to give their Telegraphic Address. Did you notice the price of the newspaper?

Bacon & Curtis sell electric fittings, but they mention this in small type at the bottom of their advertisement. They know that they will not sell very many electric fittings because so few people have electricity. Quite a lot of people still had gas in 1915 but it was used mainly for lighting. Not many people had gas stoves. What do you use gas for in your home?

Nearly everybody used coal for heating and cooking, and that is a coal-fired cooking range you can see in the advertisement. There are two ovens crammed with roasting and baking tins, there are ten pans on the top of the stove, and the plates and the gravy are keeping warm on the rack at the top.

Who is going to eat all that food?

Well, most houses would have a coal-fired cooking range like that, but this very big one is meant for a hotel.

Perhaps Bacon & Curtis fitted one of these ranges in Buckingham Palace. Anyway, they tell you proudly that they had the honour of serving King Edward VII who died in 1910.

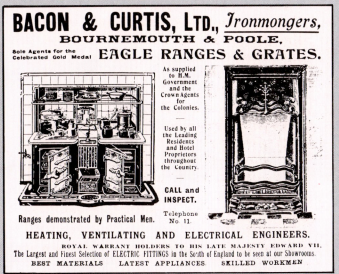

EVIDENCE

TALKING TO PEOPLE

Kings on the Run

A boy is walking along the street wearing oak leaves in his button-hole. He meets another boy who is *not* wearing oak leaves and so he stings his knees with the nettles he is carrying in his hand.

What do you suppose is happening?

Charles Stewart was born on 29th May, 1630, and he knew that he would one day be King of England. But in 1649, some of the people of England decided that they did not want a king and they chopped off the head of his father, King Charles I. The young Prince Charles escaped to France.

Charles later sailed from France to Scotland and raised an army. He marched south into England to try and win back the throne, but he was defeated at the battle of Worcester on 3rd September, 1651. After the battle he hid in an oak tree to escape from soldiers who were searching for him, and then he fled to France once more.

In the end, Charles did not have to fight for the throne. The people of England asked him to come back, and he marched into London on his thirtieth birthday.

Crowds of people lined the streets, and they wore oak leaves in their caps to remind them of the day when the king's life had been saved by oak tree leaves.

Charles Stewart hiding in an oak tree

Ever since then, 29th May has been known as Oak Apple Day, especially in the north of England, and many people wear oak leaves to show that they are on the king's side.

This is just one of the hundreds of strange customs that are to be found all over England.

On the last Sunday in August, the people of Eyam, a little village in Derbyshire, leave their churches and chapels and march out, led by a band, to a little valley called Cucklet Delf. There, they hold a special service in the open air, and the Rector preaches a sermon standing on a rock.

In 1665, thousands of people in London were dying of the plague. A parcel of cloth was sent from London to a tailor in Eyam. There must have been plague germs in the cloth, and people in Eyam soon began to die of the disease.

The Rector of Eyam, William Mompesson, told the people that if any of them left the village, or if anyone from outside was allowed into the village, the disease would spread to the country round about and thousands of people would die.

The villagers agreed to shut themselves off from the rest of the world

'Be brave!' said the Rector of Eyam

TALKING TO PEOPLE — EVIDENCE

until the plague was over. For many months they lived on food that was left for them at the edge of the village. Church services were held in Cucklet Delf so that the people would not have to touch one another.

Although 271 of the 353 people of Eyam died from the plague, no one outside the village caught the disease.

Every year, these brave people are remembered at the open air service, and a special hymn is sung that was written and sung for the first time during the plague.

England has suffered from the plague many times, and the worst plague of all was the Black Death that killed more than half of the people in England in 1350.

The village of Tissington in Derbyshire escaped the plague, and the people thought it was because the water they got from their wells was so pure.

Every year, on Ascension Thursday, the wells in Tissington are decorated with beautiful pictures made from flowers. A special service is held, and a procession marches to the blessing of each well in turn. This is the way the people remember how the village was spared 600 years ago.

The custom of decorating the wells nearly died out in 1613, and then the people of Tissington were again saved by their wells.

For more than four months, no rain had fallen over England. Wells dried up and the crops died from lack of water. Many people died from starvation. For some reason, the wells in Tissington did not dry up and the people were able to keep watering their crops. They were so thankful that they began again the custom of decorating and blessing their wells, and it still goes on today.

King Charles II was not the only king who had to hide from his enemies. It is said that, nearly 900 years ago, King Malcolm III of Scotland had to hide from the soldiers of William the Conqueror. He did this by hiding in thick bushes, and when he came out he was covered from head to foot with teazles, thistles and burrs.

On 8th July every year the Burry Man, covered with burrs from head to foot, walks through the streets of South Queensferry, near Edinburgh. At every house he visits he is greeted warmly and given gifts of food or money. This is the way the people remember how they helped King Malcolm all those years ago.

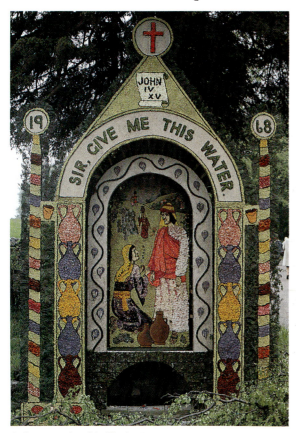

A decorated well in Tissington

The Burry Man

15

EVIDENCE

TALKING TO PEOPLE

Singers on the Roof

The customs you have read about on the last pages remind us about the great events in history. Here are some more old English customs that started with strange events that happened to ordinary people.

Sir Roger Tichborne, who owned great estates in Hampshire 800 years ago, was a cruel man. His wife, Lady Mabella, was a kind lady who always tried to help the poor people who lived in the village.

As Lady Mabella lay dying, she begged her husband to give some of his land to the villagers to grow food that could be given to the poor every year on Lady Day, 25th March.

Sir Roger laughed, and he snatched a piece of burning wood from the fire. He said he would give all the land his wife could walk around while the wood was still burning.

Although Lady Mabella was very weak, she made the servants carry her out into the fields. While the wood still burned, she crawled on her hands and knees around a piece of land as big as twenty-five football pitches, and then she was carried back to bed.

That land is still called 'The Crawls', and the corn grown on it makes about 1½ tonnes of flour every year.

Lady Mabella did not trust her husband, and before she died she made a prophecy. She said that if the Tichborne family ever stopped giving the flour to the poor, a generation of seven sons would be followed by a generation of seven daughters, and then the Tichborne name would die out.

A seventeenth century painting of the Tichborne Dole, by Giles Tilburg

TALKING TO PEOPLE

EVIDENCE

The Whitby Penny Hedge at the turn of the century

The flour was given to the poor every year for more than 600 years. In 1799, Henry Tichborne became angry with the people for fighting so noisily over the flour and he decided to put an end to the custom.

Lady Mabella's prophecy came true. Sir Henry had seven sons. When Henry Tichborne died, the estate passed to his eldest son, who had seven daughters. After that, the Tichborne name died out.

The custom was started again about 180 years ago. Every year, each man in the village receives a gallon of flour, while each woman and child receives half a gallon. It is called The Tichborne Dole.

If you go out to the beach at Boyes Staith, near Whitby in Yorkshire, on the day before Ascension Thursday, you will see something that looks rather silly.

It all started in 1159, when three hunters were chasing a wild boar. In a wood on a hill called Eskdale Side an old monk lived alone in his cell. The frightened boar ran into the monk's cell and lay trembling at his feet. The monk bolted the door of his cell and sat quietly as the hunters thrashed about in the woods outside.

At last, the hunters guessed where the boar had gone. They broke down the door of the cell, let out the boar, and beat the old man with their staves before going off on the hunt again.

The Abbot of Whitby arrived at the cell as the monk lay dying, and he heard the whole story from the old man's lips. The Abbot was very angry and wanted to have the three hunters severely punished, but the old monk made him promise not to do so.

Instead, he said that the hunters and their families should go into the woods every year for ever more and cut stakes to make a fence. The fence should be set at the edge of the sea, and it should be strong enough to stand the force of three tides.

While the stakes were being cut and the hedge planted, the Abbot's bailiff should sound his horn, read out the story of the crime, and then shout 'Out upon you!'

The fence is called the Penny Hedge. 'Penny' is short for 'penance', which is something you do when you are sorry for your behaviour.

If you should ever see this hedge being planted, do not imagine that the only people doing it are the descendants of the hunters who killed the old monk. It has become a traditional thing for all the villagers to do.

At 6 o'clock on the morning of 1st May every year, the choir of Magdalen College, Oxford, climb the steps to the top of the chapel tower and sing an old hymn to the sun in Latin. If you ask them why they do it they will say 'We have always done it!' There must be a reason, but no one knows what it is.

Magdalen College was founded by King Henry VII, and the tower was finished in 1501. The king died in 1509, and there is a story that when the choir wanted to sing a Requiem Mass for the king the chapel was not ready so they had to go up on the roof of the tower.

A detail from Holman Hunt's painting of 1891 called *May Morning on Magdalen Tower, Oxford*

EVIDENCE

1 Finding time

1. When something has been found at a dig, there are four things an archaeologist needs to know about it. Can you say what they are?

2. If an archaeologist told you that he had found in the same place a bronze spear head, a stone axe and an iron sword, which of these do you think would have been deepest in the ground?

3. Here is a drawing of a cake. It is wrapped in paper and covered with icing, so we cannot see what sort of cake it is. When it has been cut, we can see that there are layers of marzipan, chocolate, cream and jam, and the cake has lots of nuts, dates and raisins in it.

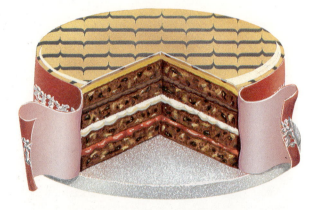

When an archaeologist digs his first trench, he can see different layers in the ground, as you can see in the other picture.

Write down the letters A to F. Against each letter, write down which of the following the archaeologist would be likely to find at that level.

Bronze tools and weapons
Stone tools and no pots
Small stone tools and pots
Anglo-Saxon brooches
A Roman paving
Iron tools and pottery

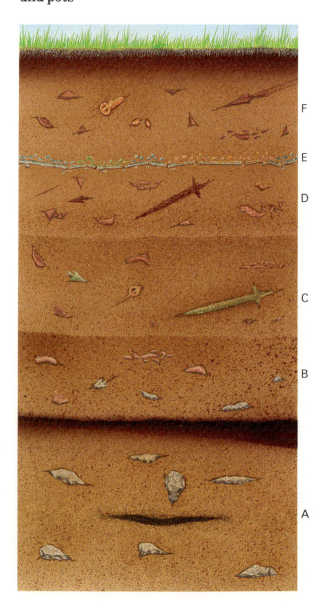

18

EVIDENCE

A Dance

A Play

4. Look at the advertisements on pages 8-9.
   a. What is a livery stable?
   b. Mr. Haydon was a Postmaster. What was that?
   c. What are (i) a landau, (ii) a dog cart, and (iii) a hack?
   d. Why did Mr. Collings sell hay and straw as well as coal?
   e. Mr. Searle made Venetian blinds. What are they? How did they get their name?
   f. Why do you think Mr. Maddock had to keep a cow?
   g. Mr. Randle sells saddles to naval officers. Why did a naval officer need a saddle?

5. Look at the things in the Harrod's catalogue.
   a. Write a short piece to tell how the Model Washing Machine worked.
   b. Explain how the Vowel Washing Machine worked.
   c. Can you think of a reason why the Barnes clothes dryer could not be used in many houses today?
   d. If you bought one of those oil lamps, you might have two other forms of lighting in your house as well. What?

6. Look at the advertisements on pages 12-13.
   a. What is a mews?
   b. Did John Walton sell ladies' hats? How do you know?
   c. How can you tell that White & Co was a large and important business? There are two clues in the advertisement.
   d. Bacon & Curtis say that they were 'Sole Agents'. What does this mean?

7.   You yourself follow many old customs, but you are so used to doing it that you have forgotten that they are customs. Pancakes on Shrove Tuesday, Hot Cross Buns at Easter, bonfires on 5th November and holly and mistletoe at Christmas are just a few. Make a list of all the customs you can think of and say how they started. Talk to old people and see if they can tell you about other customs in your town or village or in other places where they might have lived.

   Look at the two pictures here called 'A Dance' and 'A Play'. See if you can find out what these people are doing, how long people have been doing it, and how it all started.

19

EVIDENCE

LOOKING AT BUILDINGS

Stud and Mud

Between the years 400 and 1050, hardly any houses in England were built with brick or stone. They were nearly all built from wood, twigs and mud.

Here is a picture of the manor house at Lower Brockhampton in Herefordshire that was built in the year 1409. You might be surprised to know however, that this manor house is also built of wood, twigs and mud.

Why?
Because people had not found out how to make bricks?
Wrong. People had been using bricks for thousands of years.
Because the people could not afford anything better?
Wrong. The people who owned the manor house were very rich.

Lower Brockhampton Manor House in Herefordshire

In those days, when you wanted to build a house you had to find everything you needed near the place where you lived. Most of England was covered with forest, so you would not have very far to go to find the wood and twigs, and there is mud nearly everywhere.

But how do you make a house like this from wood, twigs and mud?

1. The first thing to do was to find suitable trees, chop them down and cut them into planks (called studs) to build the framework.

2. Next, wooden struts were sprung into holes drilled in the framework.

3. When all the struts were in position, willow or hazel twigs (called wattles) were woven between them.

20

LOOKING AT BUILDINGS   **EVIDENCE**

You can see that there are no gutters or drain pipes, but the roof juts out over the walls, and the upper storey juts out over the lower storey. This helped to keep the rain off the mud walls so that they did not get washed away.

Thatched roofs did not last long and they had to be mended all the time. You can see that the thatch has been replaced by tiles, and this must have been done many years after the house was built.

Houses built like this were called 'wattle and daub' or 'stud and mud'.

I wonder if the people who lived in them slept soundly on stormy nights? Or did they lie awake wondering if the walls would be washed away?

Perhaps you would not have liked to live in the manor house at Lower Brockhampton. But what about Little Moreton Hall in Cheshire? This was built of stud and mud about a hundred years after the manor house. But this house's walls were given an extra coating of lime plaster so that they could not be washed away. It made the house look more beautiful, too!

Little Moreton Hall, Cheshire

4. Very likely, the ground floor would be bare earth, but planks would be cut to make floors for the upstairs rooms.

6. Finally, the roof would be covered with a thatch of heather, reeds or straw.

5. To finish the walls, the screen of twigs was plastered with a thick layer of mud made from clay.

EVIDENCE

LOOKING AT BUILDINGS

A Long Walk

LOOKING AT BUILDINGS — EVIDENCE

The people who built the manor house at Lower Brockhampton, near Bromyard in Herefordshire, had to find all the building materials near the place where they wanted to build.

Why? Well, in those days it was almost impossible to carry heavy loads long distances from place to place. The roads were mostly nothing more than tracks cleared of trees, bushes and rocks. People travelled on foot or on horseback. Merchants carried their goods on pack horses. The roads were not good enough for carts or anything else with wheels.

When Mary I became queen in 1553 she had to travel about a lot in order to rule her kingdom properly, and she tried to travel in a horse-drawn carriage. She was shocked when she found out how bad the roads were, and she made a law that every man had to spend six days in every year working on the roads. That law was not changed until 1835.

Of course rich men often paid money instead of doing the work. But the work that was done was only filling in holes and moving fallen trees so the roads did not get very much better. It was not until about 1800 that roads were built as we know them today.

In 1580 a canal had been opened between Exeter and Bridgewater, and heavy loads were carried on the canal in barges. For nearly two hundred years this was the only canal in England. But in 1760 a group of people thought what a good idea it would be to build canals all over the country.

By 1830, thousands of miles of canals had been built at a cost of millions of pounds. But in the same year canal building suddenly stopped. The steam engine had been invented and the first railway line opened between Liverpool and Manchester. Before long, the railways had taken nearly all the traffic from the canals.

Perhaps roads are easier to build than canals or railways, but it is only in the last fifty years that we have had a network of good roads all over the country. The roads have now taken the traffic away from the railways as the railways took it from the canals.

Nowadays, it is easy to carry goods all over the country and the world. If somebody wanted to build a house in Bromyard today, the map shows some of the places the materials would come from.

Think of all the other things that would be needed: sand, putty, wallpaper, paint, taps, piping, electric wire, drainpipes, guttering, and many other things. If we were to write in the names of all the places where these other things came from our map would be full. Perhaps we would need a map of the world.

Of course, if you were a king, you could have your bricks and stones whether there were any roads or not.

In 1441, King Henry VI decided to build a new college, called King's College, at Cambridge University. He told the builders to use the best stone they could find. They told him that the best stone was to be found at Roche Abbey in Yorkshire, nearly 125 miles (200 kilometres) from Cambridge.

For many years, carts shuttled back and forth between Roche Abbey and Cambridge. Each cart carried a single block of stone. The men leading their horses were on foot. The journey over the dreadful, muddy, rutted roads took about twelve days. The men often slept under their carts at the roadside.

Eleven blocks never arrived. They disappeared completely, with the men, the horses and carts. Perhaps the men died on the way, or were killed and robbed.

One man carried twenty-seven blocks. He made the journey 54 times and must have walked more than 10,000 kilometres.

Roche Abbey, Yorkshire

EVIDENCE

LOOKING AT BUILDINGS

How Big is a Brick?

For thousands of years bricks have been the most important building material.

In your R.E. lessons you may have learnt how the Israelites became slaves in the land of Egypt. They were given clay and straw, and they had to make a certain number of bricks every day.

When Moses and Aaron asked Pharaoh to let the Israelites go, Pharaoh became very angry and gave an order for the Israelites to be punished. You can read about it in the Book of Exodus (Chapter 5, verse 6).

> *And Pharaoh commanded the taskmasters, saying: Ye shall no more give the people straw to make bricks. Let them go and gather straw for themselves.*

Perhaps you think that gathering straw is not such hard work as making bricks, but if you read on you will find that the Israelites still had to make the same number of bricks even though they had less time to do it.

All this happened more than three thousand years ago. Somebody who saw it painted a picture of the brickmakers on a wall, and if you go to Egypt you can still see the painting.

This is one of the oldest stories we have of bricks being made from clay. The bricks were not fired as they are today. Egypt is a hot country, and the bricks were laid out to bake in the sun. Straw was mixed with the clay to hold it together until it had dried.

Nowadays, bricks are heated in a furnace for many hours until they are quite hard.

Egyptians making bricks; an ancient wall painting in Thebes, Egypt

LOOKING AT BUILDINGS — EVIDENCE

Different people have had different ideas about what a brick should be like. The Romans made them long and thin – more like tiles. In the year 217, the Roman Emperor, Caracalla, had a huge bath house built from bricks in Rome. It was big enough for more than 1,600 people to bathe at the same time.

Roman bricks at Caracalla Baths, in Rome, Italy

In France, a hundred years ago, bricks were made hollow like boxes. They were much lighter than solid bricks and could be made much bigger so that fewer of them were needed to build a house.

In 1784, during the reign of George III of England, a tax was put on bricks. In order for a house to be built with fewer bricks and so cost less in tax, the brick makers started to make bricks much bigger. Some of them were so big that it took two men to lay them, one to spread the mortar and the other to lay the brick.

In 1803, the government said that double tax had to be paid on all bricks bigger than 9″ × 4½″ × 3″ (230 × 115 × 76 mm). Ever since then, bricks have been that size or smaller. So if you ever find bricks bigger than that you can be sure that they were made between 1784 and 1803.

If you ask a builder how big a brick is he will say 9″ × 4½″ × 3″, but if you go out and measure some bricks you will find that they are 8¾″ × 4³⁄₁₆″ × 2⅝″ (222 × 106 × 67 mm).

Does this mean that the builder does not know?

No. The builder has to work out how many bricks are needed for each job. If he worked out his sums with the true brick size he would get too many bricks.

Can you think why?

Roman bricks at Ostia Antica, in Italy

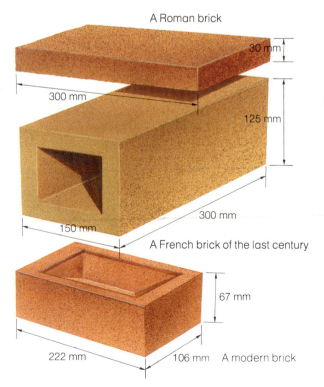

Decorative brickwork

EVIDENCE

LOOKING AT WRITING

The Royal Mail

Tom Howard had a farm in Lancashire, but he decided to sell it and buy a farm in Canada.

By 11th July, 1985, all the arrangements were complete. Tom and his wife, Brenda, said 'Good-bye' to all their friends and relations and flew off to Canada from London airport.

Nine days later, on 20th July, Brenda's mother received a long letter from Brenda to say that they had arrived safely and telling all about the new farm.

On 8th April, 1903, Arnold Baxter left England to start a new life in Australia. Arnold was only nineteen years old and his mother was very sad to see him go.

'You mustn't worry, Ma,' said Arnold. 'As soon as I get to Australia I'll write to you.'

Sixteen weeks later, on 29th July, Mrs. Baxter received a letter from Arnold to say that he had arrived safely in Australia.

Micah Clark lived in Somerset in 1663. He was a carpenter, but there was very little work for him. He had heard that a lot of people were being taken across the Atlantic free of charge to a new land called America, and he decided to go and see if he could find work there.

When he left home on 20th October, his parents knew that they would never see him again. There were no passenger ships returning from America. Even if there had been, Micah could not afford the fare.

What made it worse was that there was no post between America and England, and they would not get any letters from Micah either. When he set out to walk to Bristol he would disappear from their lives for ever.

During the voyage across the Atlantic, Micah wrote a long letter to his mother. When he left the ship in America he gave

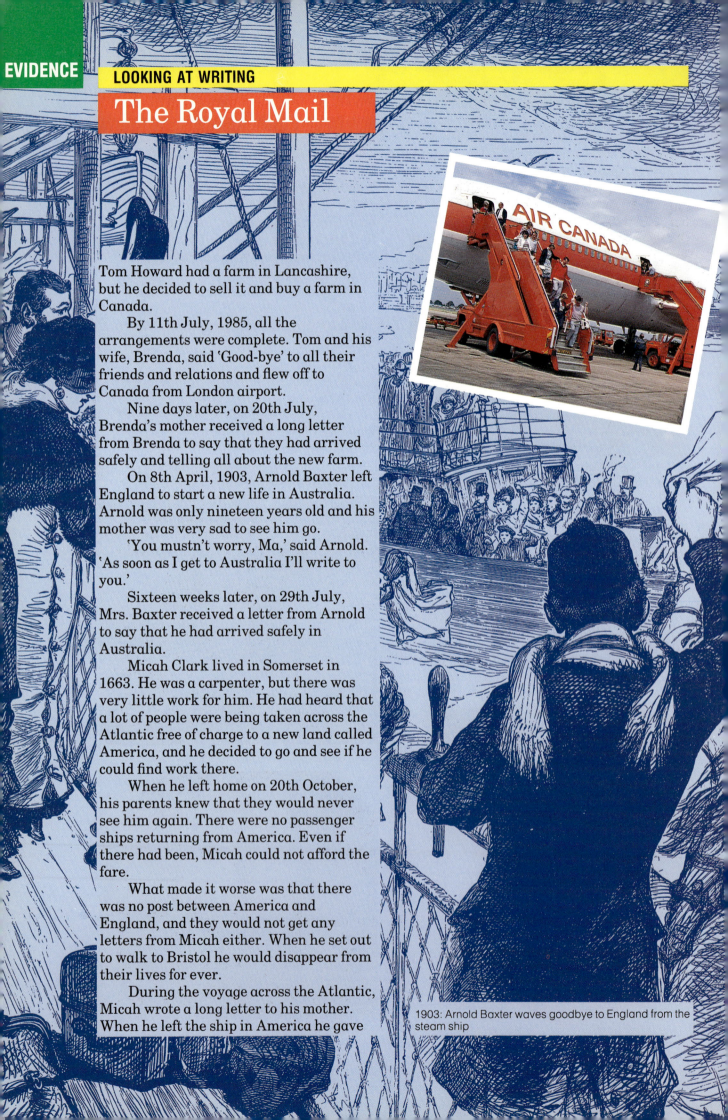

1903: Arnold Baxter waves goodbye to England from the steam ship

LOOKING AT WRITING

EVIDENCE

1663: Micah Clark hands his letter to the doomed sailor

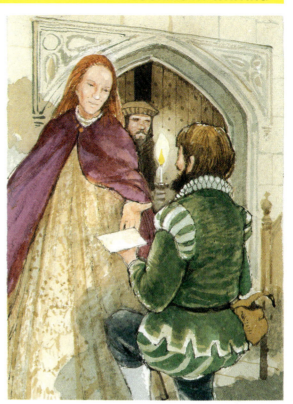

1588: William Adams kneels before Queen Elizabeth I with his urgent letter

the letter to a friendly sailor, who promised to post it when he got back to Bristol.

On the return voyage, the sailor died of scurvy. His body was buried at sea. Sailors on the ship stole his clothes and other belongings, and Micah's letter was thrown into the sea.

So Micah's parents never saw him again, nor did they ever receive any news of him.

William Adams could scarcely wait for the gangplank to be lowered before hurrying ashore from the ship that had brought him from France to England. As soon as he was safely ashore, the gangplank was raised again so that no one else could leave the ship, and William smiled grimly as he saw that the captain had carried out his orders.

It was 15th May, 1588, and William was a Queen's Messenger. In the pouch attached to his belt were urgent despatches or messages for Queen Elizabeth.

The King of Spain had assembled a great armada of ships, and these had already sailed to make war against England. William's news was that an army of about 30,000 Spaniards, led by the Duke of Parma, was waiting in Holland to cross the channel and invade England.

William carried nothing but his sword, his dagger, his purse and the despatches. He had left all his baggage on the ship so that he would be able to travel fast, and the captain had stopped anyone else from leaving the ship in case there was a Spanish agent on board who would try to stop William reaching London.

At the Blue Dolphin Inn not far from the docks was a Royal Post House, and within fifteen minutes William was galloping towards Canterbury and London. The keeper of the Post House had provided William with one of the Queen's horses, and the address of the next Post House where he could change it for a fresh one.

Seven hours later, William showed his passport to the guards at the royal palace of Whitehall, handed his seventh horse to an ostler, and was shown into an ante-room.

It was just after three o'clock in the morning, but the Queen rose from her bed as soon as she had been told that one of her messengers was seeking an audience.

It was not long before William was kneeling before the Queen to hand over his royal mail.

LOOKING AT WRITING

Second Class Post

The first postmen were King's Messengers, like William Adams about whom you read in the last story.

The household accounts of Henry III for 1259 show that he regularly paid people to carry messages, but in those days there were no special King's Messengers. The king just chose someone who was close at hand, and the man chosen had to try and find horses wherever he could along the route.

It was Henry VIII who appointed the first full-time King's Messengers in 1511. At the same time, he appointed a Master of the Posts. His job was to set up Post Houses all over the country with horses that would always be ready for the King's Messengers. The Post House was usually at an inn, but it might be at an abbey or a manor house.

The Messengers carried messages only for the King. Ordinary people could not send letters because there was no one to deliver them.

It was James I in 1608 who had the idea of letting the King's Messengers carry private letters, and you could say that this was the first official postal service.

In 1680, a man called William Dockwra started a penny post in London. In a few years he had set up more than 400 offices where letters could be handed in, and there were seven sorting offices. Letter carriers delivered the letters all over London twelve times a day.

Of course, if you wanted to send a letter to another town you had to pay a special messenger, and this would cost a lot of money.

Until 1640, the only ways to travel were on foot, cart or horseback. In 1640 the first stage coaches began to run, but they were very slow. The journey of 200 miles from London to York might take a week.

One of the original mail coaches which ran between Bath and Bristol in the eighteenth century

LOOKING AT WRITING

EVIDENCE

A Victorian letter box and a modern one

A block of unperforated Penny Blacks – the first stamps

A lot of people started giving money secretly to the coach drivers to deliver letters for them along the route, and this gave the idea for special mail coaches. In 1784, the first mail coach began to run regularly from London to Bristol, and the journey was completed in 16 hours. The horses were driven much faster, and they were changed many times along the road.

If you were in a hurry, you could travel on the mail coach, but it cost a lot more than the ordinary stage coach and it was very uncomfortable because the coach went very fast and the roads were very rough.

By 1837, William Dockwra's idea for the penny post had spread to 356 other towns all over the country, and the government set up a committee to think about starting an official postal service. A teacher of mathematics called Rowland Hill told the committee that the penny post could easily carry letters all over the country. So many people would want to send letters that all the pennies would add up to a lot of money.

The official penny post began in 1840, and for one penny you could send a letter weighing not more than half an ounce (14 grams). Gummed stamps were used for the first time, but they were printed in sheets without perforations and they had to be cut from the sheet with scissors. It was not until 1854 that perforated sheets were brought into use.

At first, all letters had to be handed in at a post office, but in 1852 the first letter boxes began to appear in the streets. They carried the Queen's monogram, as they do today. In 1852, they had VR. Now, of course, they have E II R. Some of the Victorian boxes are still in use.

In 1897, the weight that could be posted for one penny was increased to four ounces (113 grams) and, for the first time, the Post Office could promise to deliver a letter to any house in the United Kingdom.

When the postal service was started in 1837, 125 million letters were carried in the first year. In 1983 the number was more than two *billion*, and many millions of parcels were carried as well.

Nowadays, an ordinary letter costs 14p. That is thirty four of the pennies that Rowland Hill used in 1837. And that is for a second class service.

Mail is speeded across London on a Royal Mail underground train

EVIDENCE

LOOKING AT WRITING

The History of ... You?

Right: A page from a Kelly's Directory of Victorian Plymouth, and below you can see one of the streets as it might have looked

Letters are very important, and people who deliver the post have to be very honest and reliable. Even before the official postal service began in 1840 the government had appointed an Inspector of Letter Carriers. He made sure that men of good character were employed and that the service was run efficiently.

Nowadays, houses are built in neat rows called streets, and all the houses are numbered. It is easy for the postman to find your house. In those days, the postman could not always find the house, shop or office where the letter was to be delivered. Sometimes, the letter had only a name and a district.

In 1799, the Inspector had a bright idea. He got all the letter carriers to help him to make a list of all the people who lived in London, with their addresses. In 1800 he was able to have a book printed with all the names in alphabetical order, followed by the addresses.

This book was called The Post Office London Directory, and it was printed by the Inspector at his own expense. Copies were sold to the letter carriers and to anyone else who wanted one. The book was very successful and an up-to-date edition has been published every year since. You can still buy it.

LOOKING AT WRITING — EVIDENCE

In 1837, a man called Festus Frederick Kelly was appointed Inspector of Letter Carriers. In 1840 he added a trade section to the directory. All the people in the same trade were listed together. If you wanted a blacksmith near your home you could look in the trade section.

In 1841, a street section was added. Now, you could not only find where John Smith lived by looking for his name, but you could find who lived at 27 Queen Street by looking for the street.

After the government took over the postal service in 1840, the letter carriers could not help with the directory any more and Mr. Kelly gave up his job as Inspector so that he could give all his time to it. He appointed a team of agents to go round collecting the information, and after 1844 the directory was published without the help of the letter carriers.

The London Directory was so successful that Mr. Kelly started publishing directories for all the counties, and before he died in 1883 he had already begun to publish directories for the cities.

Kelly's Directories have been famous for nearly two hundred years. They are now important as history books and we can learn a great deal from them. Here are just a few things that we can learn from the trades section of the 1882 Plymouth directory.

- There were no motor cars and most transport was horse-drawn, so we find no fewer than 62 blacksmiths and harness makers.
- Not everyone had his own horse, so there is quite a list of livery stable keepers.
- Horses pull carts and carriages, so there are 16 wheelwrights.
- Very few people in those days had baths in their own homes, so there are Bath Proprietors where you could pay to have a hot bath.
- Lots of people were leaving Plymouth to go and live in Canada, Australia, New Zealand and other parts of the British Empire, so there were 7 Emigration Agents to help them.
- There are no Medical Botanists in Plymouth now. In 1882 there were five.
- Other trades that have disappeared are Clog Maker, Lamp and Oil Dealer and Tallow Chandler (maker of candles).

Every Kelly's Directory had a map of the area as well as the lists. If we compare the 1884 map of Plymouth with the 1984 map we find that the town has changed a great deal. You must remember that Plymouth suffered very badly during the last war from enemy bombing.

It may be that the public Library near you still has copies of all the Kelly's Directories for your county or town. If your family has lived there for a long time you might be able to find the name of your great great great great great great grandparents.

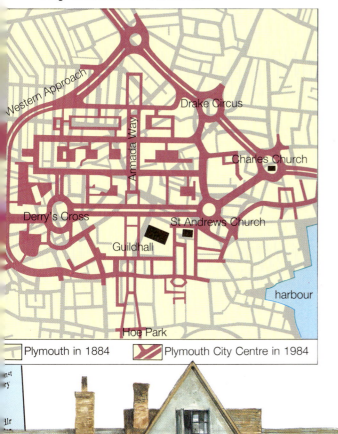

Plymouth in 1884 | Plymouth City Centre in 1984

EVIDENCE

2 *Finding time*

1. Who built houses of brick and stone in England before the year 400? Who built houses of brick and stone in England after 1050? What people invaded England between 400 and 1050? When houses were built of wattle and daub, why did the upper storey stick out over the lower storey? Try to find out if there are any houses of wattle and daub near where you live.

2. Make a list of all the things you would need if you were going to build a house just like the one you live in. Try to find out where each of them is made nowadays.

3. Here are drawings of two ways of laying bricks. Look at brick walls and make drawings of all the different ways you see. Measure the sizes of the bricks you see in the walls around you and see how many different sizes you can find.

English bond

Flemish bond

Brick is only one of the materials used in building a house

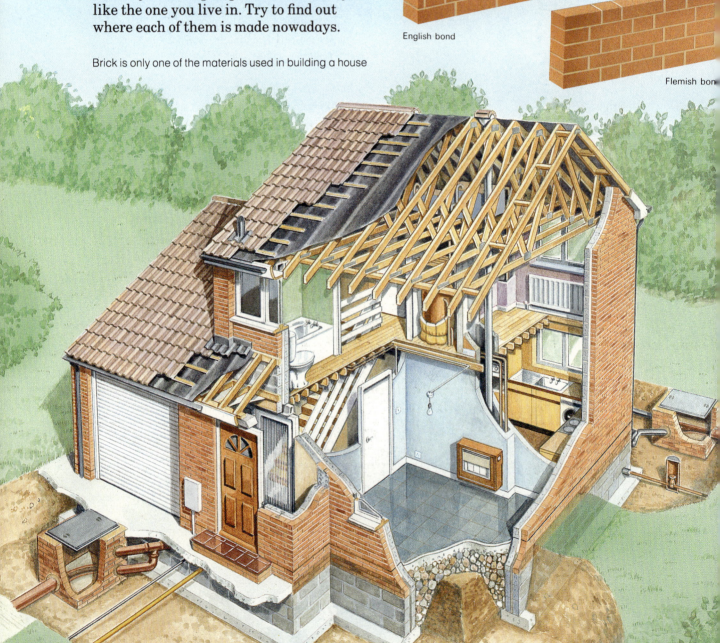

4. Sending letters
   a. Who were the very first postmen in England and what did they do?
   b. When Henry VIII appointed the first Master of the Posts, what was his most important responsibility?
   c. Who started the first penny post, and in what year?
   d. In what year did the first stage coaches start to run?
   e. In what year did the first mail coaches start to run?
   f. When would you travel by mail coach, and when by stage coach?
   g. In what year were the first gummed stamps brought into use? How were they different from the stamps we use now?
   h. Look at the pillar boxes in the town or village where you live and see what royal monogram they have.
   i. In what year did the Post Office promise for the first time that it could deliver a letter to any house in the United Kingdom?
   j. In what year was the first directory printed with all the London addresses? Why was this done?

5. Try to find a Kelly's Directory for your own town or county. If you can find one for last year and another one for twenty, thirty or more years ago, you will be able to see how your own town has changed. Make a list or chart of the changes.

Tuning a piano

6. You can see here parts of an old Kelly's Directory. There are cuttings from (a) the street directory, (b) the trade section, and (c) the commercial section in alphabetical order. See if you can find a piano tuner in all three sections.

EVIDENCE

STREET DIRECTORY.
PRETORIA ROAD.
From 54 Ladysmith road.
Map C 5.
North side.
Ladysmith Secondary Modern School for Boys (J. Turner, headmaster)
South side.
Plain Chas. G. (The Bungalow)
... here is a pass. to East av. & Polsloe rd ...

PRIESTLEY AV.
From 31 Summerway, Whipton.
Map A 7, B 7.
West side.
1 Moxey Edmund J. T
3 Josling Mrs. G. A
5 Northover Victor, piano tuner
7 Spencer Harold G
9 Gregory Ernest C. W
11 Barnett Alan
13 Davey T. R
15 Venton Wltr. T
East side.
2 Hyams Mrs. M
4 Gregory Jas. J
6 Wyatt Alonzo A
8 Dell Martin N
10 Davey Mrs. I. M
12 Spencer Kenneth G
   Padman Douglas O

TRADES DIRECTORY.
PIANOFORTE DEALERS.
See also Music & Musical Instrument Dealers.
Minns of Bournemouth Ltd. 19 Paris st
Moon & Sons (Pianos) Ltd. 192 High st

PIANOFORTE MAKERS.
Gardner P. 43f, Strand, Topsham

PIANOFORTE TUNERS
Forward L. & Son, 67 Mount Pleasant rd
Northover V. 5 Priestley av

PICTURE DEALERS.
KEETCH FRED (EXETER) LTD. (also restorers &c.), 1 Cathedral close. Tel. Exeter 74312
Samuels C. & Sons Ltd. 47 Preston st. See advert
Tudor Gallery (L. J. Smith), 93 Sidwell West street. Tel. Exeter 55395

PICTURE FRAME MAKERS.
Keetch Fred (Exeter) Ltd. (also restorers), 1 Cathedral close. Tel. Exeter 74312
Samuels C. & Sons Ltd. 47 Preston street. Telephone, Exeter 73219. See advert
Studio (The), 16 Bedford st
Urch John W. (& picture restorer), 12 West street. Tel. Exeter 55395

COMMERCIAL DIRECTORY.
NORTHCOTT & ROWE, builders & funeral directors (chapel of rest), 9 Wonford rd. & 41 & 49 St. Leonard's rd. Tel. Nos. Exeter 74565 & 59907

NORTHCOTT W. G. & CO. LTD. (regd. office), 2 Barnfield crescent. Tel. Exeter 58595/6

NORTHCOTT'S OF EXETER LTD. civil engineering contrctrs. 2 Barnfield crescent. Tel. Exeter 58595/6

Northcotts' Taxis (Mrs. F. Ley, propress.), 162 Monks rd. Telephone, Exeter 54379
Northern & Employers Assurance Group, Westminster Bank chmbrs. 246 High st. ☏ 74107/9
Northover Victor, piano turner, 5 Priestley av
Norton Cycles, cycle dlrs. 141 Fore st. ☏ 72079

NORWICH UNION INSURANCE GROUP (R. A. Brown, manager (fire & accident); E. C. Roshier, local manager (life)), Norwich Union house, 12 Bedford st. Telephone No. 74098
Norwood M. draper, 22/23 Waterbeer st. & 22 Lower Market. ☏ 72766

NORWOOD SCHOOL (R. A. Layton M.A. headmaster), 7 & 9 Pennsylvania road. Telephone 72912. See advert
Nott R. W. grocer, 48 Fore st. T. Topsham 3155
                                Wonford rd. ☏ 76591

CHANGES

SETTLING NEW LANDS

Explorers and Settlers

People have always been interested in exploring unknown places. Why do you think the people in these pictures wanted to explore these places?

Today, all of the Earth's surface has been mapped and much of it has been photographed, so explorers know a lot about the places they are going to before they get there. So if people want to go somewhere that hasn't been explored where do you think they have to go?

In the 15th and 16th centuries a lot of the world was still unexplored, and since people were curious about the world they lived in, a lot of voyages of exploration were made at this time.

You can see how much was discovered in the 15th century by comparing these two maps, one drawn in the 15th century and one drawn only a hundred years later. Write down which map you think is the earlier one and give some reasons why. Which countries were discovered after the first map was drawn but before the second one was drawn?

Two world maps drawn a century apart – which is the earlier?

SETTLING NEW LANDS

CHANGES

Some explorers were looking for new lands to settle and make their home. For over a thousand years, before 1066, Britain was explored by many different groups of people from far-off countries.

① General Julius Caesar brought an expedition to Britain to see what it was like, and what riches he could find. He landed at Richborough, Kent. The first expedition in 55BC didn't intend to settle in Britain, but they returned to Rome eager to tell everyone about the far away island. Julius Caesar wrote about it in his memoirs. Nearly a hundred years later, an army was sent to invade Britain.

② Angles and Saxon explorers made raids on British villages. After the Romans left, they came and built settlements and farmed the land. Find out where the name of England comes from.

③ Viking explorers made raids on the British coastline, plundered and returned home. But later, boatloads of men and women arrived to settle in England. They even went beyond England, and were probably the first Europeans to reach America.

④ The last invasion of Britain didn't start with exploratory raids. In 1066 the English king, Edward the Confessor, died, and the throne was claimed by a man called Harold Godwinson. But Duke William of Normandy insisted that the throne had been promised to him so he invaded England with a large army and met Harold in battle, near Hastings. Harold was killed and William marched his army to London. He set up a firm rule of the whole of England using Norman earls and barons to force the English people to obey him.

All of these settlers have left their mark on the English people, as have the Celts who were here before the Romans invaded. Since 1066, people have come from all over the world to make a home in England – from places as near as Ireland and from places as far away as the West Indies and Pakistan. All of the different settlers have contributed something different to English life. Find out which group of settlers brought the things in these pictures.

CHANGES

SETTLING NEW LANDS

Discovering America

What pictures come into your mind when you think of America? Astronauts? The President? Disneyland? Hamburgers? What else?

Until the end of the 15th century, the world that the Europeans knew was much smaller than it is today. No one knew anything about America and most people had no idea that it even existed. Most people still believed that the world was flat. In just 10 years between 1490 and 1500 the picture of the world changed when European explorers discovered South America and North America. Christopher Columbus was the first European to reach America since Leif Ericson, the Viking, had found it nearly 500 years before. But Ericson died believing that he had sailed round the world to India, and he never knew that he had found a new land. He had the right idea – he could have reached India by sailing round the world, but he didn't know that America was in the way. The world was much bigger than he realised.

The voyages of discovery were often dangerous. In 1522 an expedition set off to find a way to sail right round the world. The expedition succeeded, but only one of the five ships that set out returned, and only 18 of the 230 men who went on the expedition came home. So why did men want to go on these voyages, in unpleasant conditions, often risking their lives?

One reason was simply curiosity. Explorers who returned told stories of mountains of gold and magical herbs that would cure all illnesses, of beautiful countries, rich in wild life, with rivers full of fish and soil perfect for growing crops. People wanted to go and see for themselves and they dreamt of becoming rich. Rather like the Angles and Saxons and Vikings who made raids on England, the men who went on the first exploratory trips to North America were looking for easy wealth. One story, written in 1605, made fun of the stories that the explorers told. In the New World, 'their chamber pots are made of pure gold; all the prisoners are chained up with gold. And for rubies and diamonds, they go forth on holidays and gather 'em by the seashore to hang on their children's coats.'

The young boy (above) wanted to become a sailor and go on an expedition to the New World, but his mother wanted him to stay and farm the land like his father. What reasons would the boy give for wanting to go to sea? Why would his mother think it

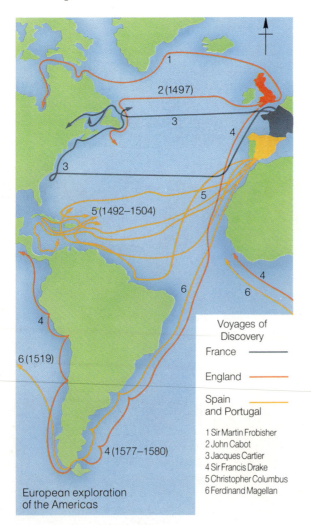

Voyages of Discovery
France ———
England ———
Spain and Portugal ———

1 Sir Martin Frobisher
2 John Cabot
3 Jacques Cartier
4 Sir Francis Drake
5 Christopher Columbus
6 Ferdinand Magellan

European exploration of the Americas

36

SETTLING NEW LANDS
CHANGES

was better for him to stay at home? Do you think she trusted the stories that were spreading about the New World?

Almost a hundred years after Columbus discovered America, Sir Walter Raleigh sent a fleet of ships to make a settlement in a part of North America which he called Virginia. The settlers were left on Roanoke Island and the ships returned to England but when another ship went back to see how the settlers were managing, the sailors found that everyone had disappeared – probably killed by natives.

American Indians helping early English settlers

Columbus called the natives of the land he found Indians – why do you think he gave them that name? What do you think the Indians felt when Englishmen landed in their country and claimed that it belonged to their queen, who lived thousands of miles away? The Indians believed that the land was like the air and the sea . . . no one could own it and no one could give it away or sell it. They weren't Christians but they believed in spirits that lived in animals and plants. Although they killed animals for food, the Indians tried not to anger their spirits by unnecessary killing.

When successful English settlements were made along the coast of North America, many of the people who came from England wanted to live peacefully side by side with the Indians. Many settlements only survived because Indians helped the settlers in the very hard first few years. How did these Indians help?

The Indians could be hostile, as the settlers in Roanoke Island found, and some settlers believed that because they were Christians, God wanted *them* to have the land and not the Indians. Many Indians were killed, and so were many English people as the Indians became frightened.

CHANGES

SETTLING NEW LANDS

Settlers – the Pilgrim Fathers

In 1620 a group of men, women and children decided to leave the security of their homes and their country and set off on a long and dangerous journey to an unknown place in North America to make a new home. Why did they take such a risk? The people who made the journey had different religious beliefs from most people in England and they wanted to live somewhere where they could bring up their children freely in the way that they believed was right. They weren't looking for gold and riches – they were willing to work hard and suffer dangers.

What do you think this family felt as they stepped onto their ship knowing that they would probably never see England again? The journey took them 66 days and once they arrived they knew that they wouldn't have much contact with home. Describe how John Billington felt – what worried him and what excited him? How did his wife Ellen feel about the journey? Frances was 14. She was longing to get to the open seas and the wild country that she had heard so much about. Describe the things that she imagined would happen to her in the next few weeks.

The Pilgrims chose to settle in a part of the New World where no Europeans had ever lived. They knew that they would have to build up their village from nothing and that it would take them some time to build houses and grow food and of course there would be no shops. Some of the things that they took with them are shown on the next page. Make a list of the things in the pictures under these headings: furniture ... utensils ... tools ... weapons ... trading goods. Who did they expect to trade with? What else might they have taken with them?

Pilgrims boarding the *Mayflower* in 1620

SETTLING NEW LANDS   **CHANGES**

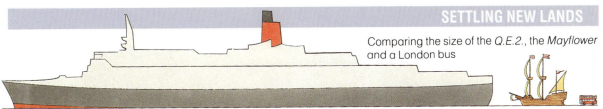

Comparing the size of the *Q.E.2.*, the *Mayflower* and a London bus

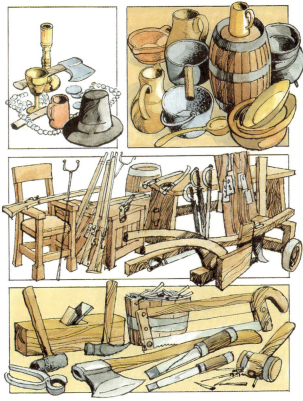

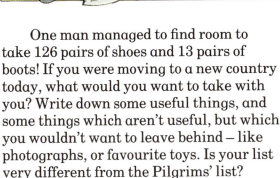

Frances' cabin in the *Mayflower*

One man managed to find room to take 126 pairs of shoes and 13 pairs of boots! If you were moving to a new country today, what would you want to take with you? Write down some useful things, and some things which aren't useful, but which you wouldn't want to leave behind – like photographs, or favourite toys. Is your list very different from the Pilgrims' list?

This picture shows you how big their ship the *Mayflower* was compared with the QE2 which makes the Atlantic crossing to New York today. Today, safety regulations allow a ship the size of the *Mayflower* to carry crew only and no passengers. In 1620, there were over 100 passengers on the *Mayflower*. Most of the passengers spent a lot of the journey crowded together in one cabin where they had to sleep, eat, dress, wash, prepare food and look after the children. Why was it especially uncomfortable for adults even if they weren't very tall?

Can you find where Frances and her family slept in the cabin? Write a page of Frances' diary – describe the cabin, the smells after a few weeks when most of the passengers had been seasick and hadn't been able to bath. Describe the noise that so many people crowded together would make. Describe what the passengers did all day long, especially if it was too rough to go up on deck. Describe the damp that they couldn't keep out of the cabin, and the continual noise of the wind, the water on the side of the ship, the sails and the creaking of timbers.

Why couldn't the passengers on the *Mayflower* have fresh food to eat? The water wasn't very safe to drink, so most people drank beer and sometimes wine. They ate meat and fish that had been smoked or salted to stop it from going bad but they had very few vegetables so by the end of the journey most people were weak from their poor diet, from being crowded together below deck, and from seasickness. In this condition, they had to find somewhere suitable to build a village and they had to make shelters for themselves against the bitter wintry weather which was already beginning.

CHANGES

SETTLING NEW LANDS

Making a New Home

When the Pilgrims reached the coast of North America after over two months at sea, they had no time to rest and recover from the journey before they tackled the vast job in front of them. One of the men on the *Mayflower*, William Bradford, described their arrival like this: 'they had no friends to welcome them nor inns to entertain or refresh their weatherbeaten bodies; no houses or much less towns to repair to ... what could they see but a hideous and desolate wilderness, full of wild beasts and wild men ...'

They knew that they couldn't return to England as most of them were too weak to survive another journey like the one that was thankfully over now.

They arrived in New Plymouth on Saturday December 9th, 1620. Use these pictures to write some entries in Frances' diary for the few weeks after they arrived. Include the answers to these questions in the diary:

1. Why didn't they go and explore on the first day that they arrived?
2. What did the men do?
3. What did the women do?
4. What did the children do?
5. What did they find to eat? What other useful things did they find near the settlement?
6. What was their first contact with the Indians like?

The Pilgrims arrived at the worst possible time of the year – just as the winter was setting in. Today we don't think of winter as being dangerous, but the danger was very real for the Pilgrims. By March, four months after they had

40

SETTLING NEW LANDS

CHANGES

arrived, half of the people who had left England had died. Why did so many get ill and die?

The seeds which the Pilgrims brought with them from England didn't grow very well. But as they became friendly with the Indians, they were shown how to grow 'Indian corn' or maize, which grew very well. At the end of their first summer the Pilgrims held a Thanksgiving feast. Today in the U.S.A., Thanksgiving feasts are still held in most homes on the fourth Thursday in November. Imagine that you are the new governor of the Pilgrim's settlement, which they called New Plymouth. Make up a speech of thanksgiving to open the first celebrations, which they held in October 1621.

The first Thanksgiving feast

CHANGES

3 Finding time

1. Why would this photograph help someone who wanted to make a map of the area? What do you think 15th and 16th century map makers used instead of photographs?
2. Why did all the early invaders and settlers arrive in England by boat? How did these settlers arrive in England in 1984? They had to pass through Immigration Control – find out what this is. What did these immigrants or settlers have to have which the early settlers didn't have?

The coastline of Cornwall seen from a satellite

CHANGES

3. Look at the map on page 36 and then explain why Spanish is the main language spoken in South America today, while in North America English is the main language.

North American signs, in English

South American signs, in Spanish

4. How would these things have helped the Pilgrims when they landed in America? What did they have instead of each thing in the picture?

5. The only contact with home that the Pilgrims had was through the ships that arrived from England, usually not more than once a year. They could send letters to their families and letters from home came on these ships. What contact with England can people in America have today?

6. The new settlement that the Pilgrims built was named after the town that the *Mayflower* had sailed from in England – Plymouth. William Bradford said the Pilgrims wanted their children to know that they were descended from Englishmen who 'came over the great ocean, and were ready to perish in this wilderness.' Can you find the names of any other English towns on the map of the area around New Plymouth?

CHANGES

FINDING OUT ABOUT THE WORLD

The Medieval Picture of the World

Medieval travellers embarking on a voyage

Can you picture the shape of Britain in your mind? Do you know whether the world is flat, round or a cylinder? Is the world held up by gravity, elephants or turtles? Is it surrounded by sea, air, clouds or empty space? These seem like simple questions today, because we have many

ways of finding out about the world. Name the things in this picture which are numbered, and explain why each thing helps us to get a broad picture of the world.

In the Middle Ages, people asked all sorts of questions about the world they lived in – but why weren't the answers easy to find?

Why was it harder to travel far and see the world?

Why was it harder to share information about the world before there were cheap printed books, and when few people could read?

Would this map of the world have been much use to medieval travellers setting off into the unknown?

This map dates from about 1300 and is one of the oldest in the world. The artist put Jerusalem at the centre of the world and Britain was shown on the very edge

FINDING OUT ABOUT THE WORLD — CHANGES

The medieval map shows the world surrounded by oceans. The map-maker, like most people at that time, believed that the world was flat. Some people thought that the world was round, but the only way to prove it was to try to sail right round the world . . . and what if they were wrong? The men who sailed with Christopher Columbus were frightened in case they sailed right off the edge of the world . . . and what might they fall into?

As travelling was slow and often dangerous, many medieval villagers didn't move far away from their home village, so the world they knew was very small. They were most interested in local news . . .

Visitors to Bampton were rare in the Middle Ages so they were greeted with great excitement and they were asked to tell stories about their travels – then the stories were told and retold by villagers on winter evenings. In this way, the medieval villager pieced together a picture of far-off parts of the world.

This stonemason helped build the massive cathedral at York.

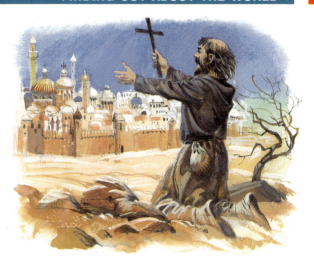

This pilgrim has travelled across Europe to Jerusalem.

This soldier has come back from fighting in France.

This pedlar has stories of a terrible plague which destroyed most of the people living in one village.

Using the pictures to help you, make up a story for each traveller to tell. Make them exciting – you might be the only visitor for months!

45

CHANGES

FINDING OUT ABOUT THE WORLD

Scribes and Storytellers

Can you imagine what it would be like if hardly anyone could read? Every time you go out in the street, you see written words all around you, but if people couldn't read there would be no point in having the words. Describe what this busy street would be like without any written words — what might you have instead of newspapers... road signs... advertising posters?

In the Middle Ages, all books were written by hand. They were very expensive, so as you saw in Book 2 only wealthy people, universities and monasteries could afford to buy them. Most books were copied out by monks as you can see in the picture below. It might take six months to copy just one book.

1. Why do you think it was forbidden for monks to have candles or even fires in the room, when they were copying books? Describe what it must have been like in winter when monks had to write for 6 hours every day.
2. Explain why you think one monk wrote 'Thank goodness, thank goodness, thank goodness' at the end of his book!
3. Why were the manuscripts chained up?

The books were written on parchment which is made from animal skins and the scribe couldn't rub out his mistakes as you can on paper. The books were harder to read than books with clear printed words like the one you are reading now, and monks were allowed to borrow library books for a year. How long can you keep the books from your local library?

Some valuable books were secured by chains

46

FINDING OUT ABOUT THE WORLD

CHANGES

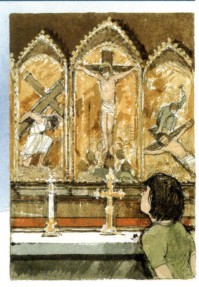

In the Middle Ages, most children in England didn't go to school and so most people couldn't read or write. Describe how the children in these pictures are learning without books. What kind of books would you look at to learn these things today?

As most people couldn't read, anyone who could tell a good story was always popular and would draw a big crowd. This group of actors travelled around acting out stories in town squares and inns. Sometimes the stories came from the Bible ... sometimes they described real events, events from history or things which had happened recently ... and sometimes they were just good stories! What story are they acting out here to the villagers of Bampton?

Medieval players in the market square

CHANGES

FINDING OUT ABOUT THE WORLD

Spreading the Word

The book that you are reading now obviously wasn't written by hand. How can you tell? In 1476, William Caxton brought the first printing press to England. Within a few years there were many more books in the world because printed books could be produced much more quickly and cheaply than hand-written books. Who could share the discoveries which people made about the world after they were printed in books?

In this picture of an early printing shop, you can see how books were printed not long after Caxton's death. The workers are finding the metal letters and laying them in a composing stick, then each line of type is tipped into a metal tray which is the same size as the page. When the page is laid out, the letters are inked and fixed into the press. The paper is put on top of

This woman is reading a book made over 400 years ago. What is the oldest book you've ever read?

FINDING OUT ABOUT THE WORLD

CHANGES

the letters and then a weight is brought down onto the pages.

1. One man is inking the pages. What are the inking-balls like?
2. How is the paper carried into the shop?
3. How is the ink on the printed paper dried?
4. How do the printers work the press?
5. Why do you think the letters in the composing stick are the wrong way round?
6. Where does the light in the printing shop come from?

Many of the early manuscripts were very beautifully written, with detailed and careful illustrations, and some people felt that the printed books were poor copies. Printers tried to make their books look like manuscripts but some wealthy people actually employed scribes to copy printed books out by hand!

Of course printed books were only useful to people who could read them. Many of the early books were written in Latin, not in English, and they were mainly religious books or chronicles of events happening at the time.

Then books were printed on a much wider range of subjects, and in English. Who do you think would have read these early books? How did they help people to find out about the world they lived in? Which books in your classroom or library help you to find out about the world that *you* live in?

But for many people things changed very slowly. Three hundred and fifty years after books were first printed, most people lived in the countryside and worked on the land – they didn't go to school and they had no books in their houses. More than half the population couldn't read. Even though books had become cheaper they were still too expensive for most people.

In 1870 a law was passed which said that all children must go to school. Once most people could read the world started to fill up with written words. Today we take for granted all the writing that we see about us. What written words did people see around them 100 years ago? What are the posters below advertising? What else is happening in the picture?

How are Victorian advertisements different to ours?

CHANGES

FINDING OUT ABOUT THE WORLD

The Shrinking World

Today, news reports can be sent across the world almost instantly. How are these reports being sent? In the past, news could only travel as fast as the fastest means of transport.

1066 'Duke William of Normandy invades and claims the throne of England!' This news report took 5 days to reach King Harold in York, about 250 miles away. How do you think the news travelled?

1805 'Nelson killed in battle!' 17 days later this news was reported in *The Times* in London. How was the news carried? Until the 19th century, it was hard to find out about events taking place across the world. The fastest way to travel across land was on horseback, and travel by sea was slow because ships were dependent on currents and winds to carry them. The arrival of the railway meant that people could travel faster than ever before and the new steam ships helped to open up the world.

Royal Mail's steamship *Scotia* in the nineteenth century. Would it go faster than the *Mayflower*? If so, why?

FINDING OUT ABOUT THE WORLD

CHANGES

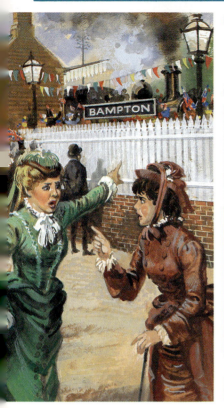

When Annie Parry was growing up, the village of Bampton hadn't changed a great deal since the Middle Ages. Then in 1873 a railway station was opened and Annie was worried about the effect that it would have on the village. Emmie Parks was pleased that the railway had come, as she thought that it would put Bampton in touch with the rest of the country. With a friend, argue Annie's view that the railway will spoil the village, and Emmie's view that it will help develop the village.

Today, a lot of stations have been closed. In many villages there is less public transport than there was when Annie and Emmie were alive. Although this makes things difficult for some people, it isn't as hard as it used to be for villagers to keep in touch with the outside world. Six things which help this family to 'keep in touch' today have been taken out of the picture, but clues have been left. Can you name the missing things?

Would you like to fly on Concorde? Find out where it can take you and for how much

51

CHANGES

4 *Finding time*

1. In the Middle Ages, stories about far-off countries were often a mixture of truth and fantastic legends. People loved to hear stories of strange creatures from mysterious, undiscovered parts of the world. Why was it hard for people to tell what was truth and what was fantasy in the stories? Which undiscovered places do strange creatures in stories often come from today? Here are some monsters for you to draw.

CHANGES

2. *News Flash!* Match each item of news with the correct picture to find out how the news was spread.

1415　*King Henry V triumphant at Agincourt!*
1606　*Plot to blow up Parliament fails. Trial of conspirators starts tomorrow.*
1939　*War is declared against Germany.*
1986　*Nuclear disaster at Chernobyl, Russia.*

3. How would it have been different for the Pilgrims if the *Mayflower* had been a steamship? What other things have changed which make far-off countries seem nearer? The MacPherson family are emigrating to Australia. It is 1984. Describe how they plan their journey. How do they find out what it is like in Australia? How do they find out how they can travel, the cost of tickets and the length of the journey? How do they get in touch with relations in Australia before they go, and friends in England after they settle in Australia?

Compare the MacPherson's journey with these men, who are about to set off on a long sea voyage across the world, with Captain Cook, but they don't know exactly where they are going. It is 1768. No one knows how long the journey will take, nor what they will find when they get there – if they get there, for the journey is dangerous. Describe how the sailors might feel. Are they excited, or frightened? What do they imagine that the next few months will have in store for them? Will they miss their families? Will they be able to keep in touch with them?

53

CHANGES

MEDICINE AND HEALTH

Clean and Healthy

Life in England used to be much more dangerous than it is today, although we often feel now that we live in a dangerous world... What do your parents warn you about?

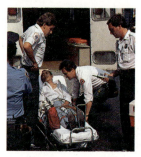 

Until just over a hundred years ago, one of the main dangers that people had to cope with was illness and disease. It had taken many hundreds of years for people to realise just how many illnesses were due to lack of hygiene and cleanliness. The danger was so great that a lot of children used to die before they were 5 years old – babies from rich and poor families. Queen Anne (1702–14) had 6 children, but they all died very young.

What is this mother doing to make sure that there are no harmful germs on her baby's bottle? Why is it so important to keep babies' things very clean?

When babies are born, they have just spent 9 months growing in the safe protected world inside their mother's body. Suddenly they emerge into a world where there are germs which can make people ill. As we get older our bodies learn to protect themselves against many of these germs, but new-born babies don't have much protection, so the mother has to keep the germs away from the baby.

This mother had her baby in 1783. She thought that the baby would be made ill by bad smells carried in the air, so she never opened the window. There was no special baby milk then, so unless the babies had their mother's milk, they were given bread soaked in water with sugar, or perhaps cow's milk, which we now know can make new-born babies ill. How many children did this woman have? If several of them were crying at once and she was tired, she sometimes gave them gin to send them to sleep.

Using the picture and information above, describe some of the dangers that a new-born baby had to face in the 18th century. Why didn't the baby get any fresh air? Why is fresh air important? What did the baby have instead of a bottle? Why wasn't it hygienic?

MEDICINE AND HEALTH

CHANGES

When you turn on a tap, where does the water that gushes out come from? How do you know that it is clean and safe to drink? Why shouldn't you drink river water?

In the Middle Ages, toilets were often built directly over rivers, and chamber pots were emptied straight into rivers and streams. Then the dirty river water often mixed with water that people drank, which gave them illnesses like dysentery and fevers.

In 1348, a terrible plague, which people called the Black Death, killed thousands and thousands of people all over Europe. No one knew what caused the plague, but some people believed that contaminated water (water with harmful germs in it) might be to blame. In some places people started to empty their toilets into huge holes called cess pits instead of into the river. But in the towns especially the cess pits were very unpleasant, because there were so many people crowded together with little space between the houses. Cess pits often contaminated drinking water under the ground, so no one could see the danger.

In the 19th century, towns started to grow very quickly as people crowded together to find jobs in the new factories, and new houses and tenements were put up without proper planning, and without enough toilets or taps for water. Why do you think that the people who were in a position to change things often moved out to the more pleasant suburbs?

These Victorian houses also had toilets emptying into the river

Building a sewer in London in 1845

This cartoon of 1858 was captioned: *Father Thames introducing his offspring* (Diptheria, Scrofula, Cholera) *to the fair city of London*

In 1832, a dangerous illness appeared in England which attacked rich and poor alike. In 1854 John Snow discovered that this illness, called *cholera*, was passed on through polluted drinking water. This fact frightened people in authority into making the changes that were needed. Sewerage systems were built to empty toilets safely away from drinking water, and authorities were set up in towns to make sure that pipes were laid to carry clean water safely to many houses. It took many years before water was piped to every house.

CHANGES

MEDICINE AND HEALTH

Going to the Doctor

What is your doctor like? Can you find some good words to describe him or her? Do any of these descriptions fit your doctor? 'He has magical powers', 'He is savage', 'She collects plants for her medicines from the fields and hedges', 'God gave him power to heal people.'

In the Middle Ages, most people couldn't afford to go to trained doctors or to buy their medicine from apothecaries. In villages, many women believed that God had provided a plant to cure every illness. They said that they knew which herbs would cure headaches, which plants would reduce fevers, and which plants were useful for healing wounds. In this picture you can see one woman who had special healing powers, and the women in this village turned to her if their herbs didn't work, or if they had an unusual illness. Where do you think she went to get the herbs that she used? How do you think she knew which plants to use? This woman frightened some of the villagers as they didn't understand her powers – they didn't know if God gave her the power to heal . . . or if she might be a witch with evil powers.

People have always used some herbal medicines and they are still used today. One of the largest chain stores in England, *Boots* the chemist, started as a shop selling herbal medicines, in the 1850's. When the shop first opened, Jesse Boot saw patients in a back room and sold some of these things in the shop: sage (for sore throats) elderflower and peppermint (for colds) comfrey (for mending broken bones and healing wounds) mustard powder (for coughs and colds).

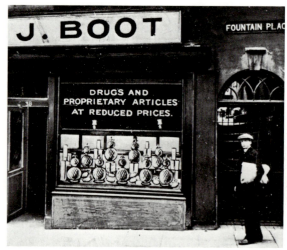

The first *Boots* – at Goose Gate, Nottingham

Can you buy the same things in *Boots* today? What else do they sell?

Do you know how many years training doctors must have before they can take on patients? See if you can find out. No one is allowed to practise as a doctor until they have passed exams and had their name put on a register of trained doctors. But before 1815, finding a good doctor in the towns was largely a matter of luck. Anyone could practise as a doctor, even without training, and although there were some very good doctors who trained themselves, there were also a lot of 'quacks' – people who knew that their medicines were useless, but they sold them to make money for

MEDICINE AND HEALTH — CHANGES

themselves. In the 18th century one quack sold medicines which would stop people from getting these illnesses: 'The Strong Fives, The Wambling Trot, The Marthambles, The Moon-Fall and the Hockogrockle'. No one who took his medicine did get these made up illnesses ... so do you think they worked?

This dentist is going to fill a cavity in a tooth. What is he doing to stop it from being painful?

The dentist is injecting a *local anaesthetic*. It stops the pain in one place. Surgeons often give *general anaesthetics* to their patients before they operate, to make them unconscious so that they won't feel any pain.

What was it like before surgeons had anaesthetics? People had experimented for hundreds of years to try to find pain killers, but it wasn't until 1799 that Humphry Davy found a gas called nitrous oxide which stopped patients from feeling pain while they had an operation. In the middle of the 19th century, two other substances were found which worked as anaesthetics: ether and chloroform. A lot of people were worried about using anaesthetics as they seemed 'unnatural' but after Queen Victoria used chloroform when she had one of her babies in 1847, it became much more widely used. Why do you think people thought it was unnatural to use anaesthetics?

A Victorian doctor visiting a young patient

Before anaesthetics were discovered, operations were so painful and dangerous that they were only performed if there was no other chance of saving the patient's life. Physicians didn't perform the operation, but they employed barber-surgeons who were much less respected. The barber-surgeons were often rough, uneducated men who had to be very strong – no one else wanted to do such a terrible job. You can see what the conditions were like in the picture.

1. The surgeon had to work very fast, so he couldn't be very careful. Why did he have to work so fast?
2. What is the barber-surgeon wearing in his hat?
3. Why is the patient struggling?
4. Explain why very few patients survived major operations.
5. Find out how long heart transplant operations take today. Why would they have been impossible before the discovery of anaesthetics?

A barber-surgeon

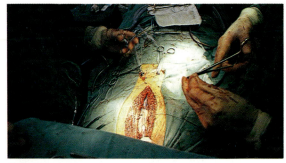

Open heart surgery

CHANGES

MEDICINE AND HEALTH

New Discoveries

How can doctors tell what is wrong with their patients? Can you tell what is wrong with the patients in this waiting room? Some illnesses show on the outside of the body, but some people only know that they are ill because they feel sick, or dizzy or have pains somewhere. How do doctors know what is happening *inside* the body?

Before doctors understood the causes of illnesses, their 'cures' sometimes worked, but they often didn't work very well. In the Middle Ages, some people believed that illnesses were sent by God as a punishment for sins, or that evil spirits had invaded the body. As well as going to doctors, some people believed that priests and magicians could cure the sick, and the king was believed to have special powers to cure a disease called scrofula. During the plague outbreak in 1665, no one knew that it was caused by a type of flea which lived on rats. Some plague victims turned to doctors, some turned to priests, and some turned to magicians. The doctor (below) had spices in the beak, which he believed would stop the infected air from reaching him. The wand meant that he could take a patient's pulse without touching him. Which one would you trust if you were ill – the doctor, the priest, or the magician?

When the printing press came to England in 1476, a lot more text books on medicine were soon available. Discoveries that doctors made about the human body could be passed on to other doctors, but also people could spread fantastic ideas about healing and medicine which often confused doctors instead of helping.

Until the 18th century, it was against the law for doctors to dissect dead bodies to find out how the organs inside the body work. Some people broke the law and there were a few very good books on the anatomy of the human body, but there were also books with wrong information. Why was it so important for doctors to know what the inside of the body is like?

Some plague victims turned to a doctor, some to a priest, and some to a magician

MEDICINE AND HEALTH | CHANGES

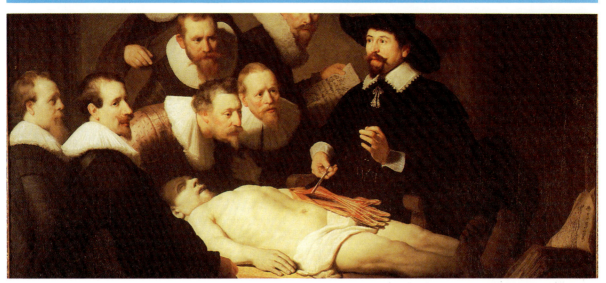

The Anatomy Lesson, painted by Rembrandt in the seventeenth century

During the 18th century, doctors were allowed to dissect the bodies of executed criminals, but there weren't enough bodies for all medical students to be able to study anatomy properly. Describe this anatomy lesson. Do you think that the students learnt much? In 1832 a law was passed allowing doctors to study the bodies of people who died a natural death, and student doctors were able to learn a lot more.

Another great advance which helped doctors discover how the body works was the discovery of X-rays in 1895. Why did X-rays help doctors? What can you see on these X-ray pictures?

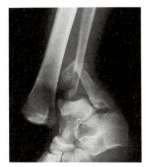 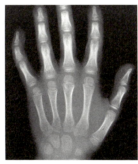

One way that knowledge spread was through doctors trying out new ideas for cures on their patients and seeing if they worked. Of course, this could be dangerous.

Smallpox used to be a common illness which was very unpleasant and often very dangerous until, in 1796, Edward Jenner discovered a way of protecting people against the disease. He gave a healthy 8 year-old boy a vaccine, which was a mild dose of the germs which caused cowpox, a similar illness.

Then the boy's body built up antibodies which protected him when Jenner later injected him with smallpox. If the vaccine hadn't worked, the boy could have died of smallpox.

The same method is used to protect people against many infectious diseases today. When you were a baby, you were probably vaccinated against illnesses which used to be common, but are rare now, because of the vaccinations. Smallpox is unheard of now, throughout the world. Find out which vaccinations you have had.

A statue of Jenner's famous experiment

CHANGES

MEDICINE AND HEALTH

Going to Hospital

In the early 18th century, there were only two hospitals in the whole of London. Usually, doctors visited patients in their own homes. Who else helped the sick before Henry VIII closed the monasteries in the 1530's? Describe the rooms that the sick were kept in. Before people realised the importance of hygiene in preventing illness, it was much safer to be ill at home than at hospital. This description of a hospital was written by Florence Nightingale less than 150 years ago:

'The nurses did not as a general rule wash patients . . . The beds on which the patients lay were dirty. It was common practice to put a new patient into the same sheets used by the last occupant of the bed, and mattresses were . . . sodden and seldom if ever cleaned.' Another nurse told Florence Nightingale that 'she had never known a nurse who was not drunken . . .'

Miss Nightingale was so horrified at what she saw in hospitals that she set up a school to train nurses and she wrote a handbook for student nurses. She wrote about the importance of cleanliness, fresh air, clean water and plenty of light. What would you have felt if you had been taken to this hospital in the middle of the 19th century? Write about some of the things that you would want to see changed and say how things could be improved. Compare the picture of the hospital in 1845 with the picture of a hospital ward today. Describe some of the things that have changed. Find out about Florence Nightingale's work during the Crimean War and how she helped to improve conditions in hospitals.

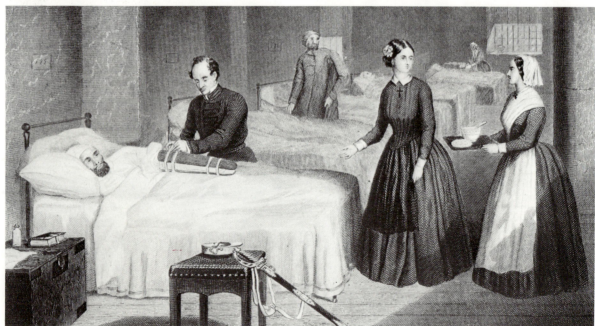

Florence Nightingale at work

MEDICINE AND HEALTH

CHANGES

You saw how painful operations were before the discovery of anaesthetics. Patients who didn't die of shock faced another danger from the dirty conditions. People often died from simple operations such as setting a broken leg, because the wound would become infected and the infection would spread. The instruments that surgeons used were often dirty and they may not have been cleaned since they were used to operate on an infected wound. In 1865, Joseph Lister discovered that if instruments, clothing, the surgeon's hands and the wound itself were sprayed with an antiseptic, carbolic acid, this stopped infections from setting in. It took a long time before his ideas were accepted, as people thought that infections came from bad smells, not from bacteria in the air and instruments in the operating theatre. These two pictures show how much has changed in just over 100 years.

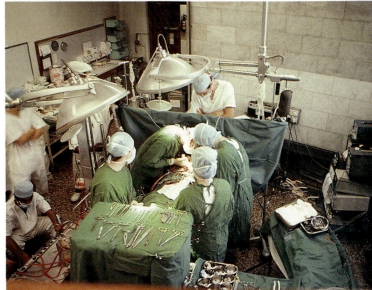

An operating theatre in 1890, and below in 1980

Very early operating instruments

A modern hospital ward

61

CHANGES

5 Finding time

1. How have these things helped to make life safer for new-born babies?

2. Describe a situation when the things in these pictures were important in saving lives. What did people do before they had these things?

3. Another name for the anaesthetic nitrous oxide is laughing gas. Why do you think it was given this name? How did these people find out that laughing gas was a pain-killer?

CHANGES

4. Jenner experimented on an 8 year-old boy. His experiment worked and he saved the lives of thousands of people who might have died of smallpox. Today, no one is allowed to try out new drugs on patients until they have been tested on animals and found to be safe. Many people feel that it is cruel to test drugs on animals – others say that if the drugs aren't tried out on animals, then we will never find the new drugs that we need. It is a very complicated problem. Talk to your parents or teachers, and to your friends and try and decide what you think.

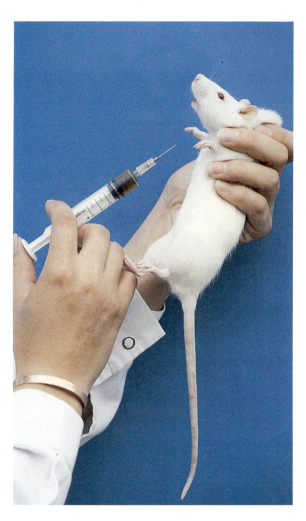

5. In China, people used to pay their doctors when they were well, and if they became ill, they were treated free of charge. Do you think that this is a good idea?

6. Why do you think that surgeons became more respected and skilful after anaesthetics and antiseptics were used in operations? When have you seen these antiseptics (right) used?

7. Look again at the operating theatres on page 61, and then answer these questions:

1980's

a. Why are the surgeons wearing gloves and masks?
b. How is the operating theatre lit?
c. The air in the operating theatre is specially filtered to purify it. Why is this done?
d. Find out what the machines on the right are for.

1890's

e. Who are the people watching?
f. What is the nurse on the left cleaning?
g. Why was it dangerous for the patient to have so many people watching the operation?
h. Describe the clothes that the surgeons wore.
i. How is the operating theatre lit?
j. Which theatre would you prefer, and why?

63

PROJECT

ENTERTAINMENT

Playtime

Which ending would you be most likely to give to this sentence? 'I can't come and have tea yet, I'm busy...

...putting the falcon away.'
...polishing my sword.'
...making a snowman.'
...playing in the moon craters.'
...watching television.'

Do you have enough time to play? Do you wish that the summer holidays would never end, or do you get bored and want to go back to school? Write a list with some of the things that you would do now if your teacher told you that you could have the day off school. Which of the things on your list could a child have done a hundred years ago, or more? Remember, there was no electricity, or plastic to make toys. What were children's toys made of before plastic?

Eighteenth-century toys

ENTERTAINMENT · PROJECT

Drury Lane Theatre in 1894

A piano recital at the end of the last century

Charles Dickens giving a public reading of his stories in 1861

Modern entertainment. How have things changed?

Is it just children that play? What kinds of things do adults do when they aren't working? Television keeps a lot of people entertained for a lot of the day. Sometimes, on a cold wintry night it can be much more comfortable to be entertained at home than to have to wrap up and go outside. But why is it sometimes more enjoyable to go out and have fun? Which programmes can you watch today if you want to hear music? . . . if you want to watch sport? . . . if you want to laugh? . . . if you want to see a good play or hear a good story? Describe how people 150 years ago might have watched the same thing.

Childen have always played imaginative games, where they pretend to be different and exciting people. Do you ever pretend to be space explorers on new planets? Do you imagine that you are driving fast cars – perhaps cars with special powers – or fast motorbikes? Who did children in the past pretend to be, in the days before there were people in space and fast cars? Describe the games that these children are playing.

PROJECT

ENTERTAINMENT

'Once upon a Time...'

Listening to stories on television, on the street, and in school

Do you like reading stories to yourself or do you like listening to someone reading out loud? When you get to secondary school, you will probably find that teachers don't read out loud to you – you will be expected to read to yourself, like adults. But is storytelling just for children? In a lot of warm countries where people can spend more time outside – such as Morocco in North Africa – storytellers sit in the streets. They tell stories to adults and children and, in the past, this used to happen in England too. When do people tell each other stories today?

Minstrels used to be important entertainers in England in the days before there were printed books, and before there were real theatres. There weren't many books and so the minstrels travelled around the countryside taking with them exciting stories, poems, and music as well as news of interesting events. Why was it important for the minstrels to have a good memory?

The minstrels were welcome almost everywhere. When Edward I's daughter was married, there were 426 minstrels to entertain the wedding guests. But minstrels also stayed in the simple poor homes of peasants, telling stories and singing songs in return for a bed and food.

66

ENTERTAINMENT

Some minstrels joined groups of travelling entertainers, who performed at village fairs, or in town market places. You can see that there was other entertainment as well as storytelling.

1. Describe the place where this group of entertainers performed.
2. What are the different entertainers doing to amuse the crowd?
3. Choose three of the people in the crowd and say what you think they were doing before the entertainers arrived, and what they will do after the players have gone.
4. How did the players make their money? Do you think they made as much money in winter as in summer?
5. How did they travel? How are things easier for this group of travelling entertainers today?

Medieval entertainers – perhaps the minstrel is singing a story

A pop group on tour

The minstrels often chanted their stories or sang them and played an instrument such as a lute. They sang ballads about wars and heroes from the past, or stories of love. They told stories to make their audience laugh, and they told stories from history in an entertaining way. People loved to hear stories of Robin Hood, the rebel who boldly robbed the rich, but was kind to the poor. Do any pop singers today tell good stories in their songs?

Find out about an exciting event which happened not too long ago. Make up a story or a song using the information that you have found. (You can use newspapers, books, or talk to your parents, teachers or friends). Then tell your story or sing your song to the class or to your friends. Make it exciting or funny so that your audience will enjoy it.

PROJECT

67

PROJECT

ENTERTAINMENT

A Pilgrim Storyteller

PROJECT

ENTERTAINMENT

On the Road

Who was the Nun's Priest who told the story of Chanticleer and Pertelote?

At the end of the fourteenth century – about a hundred years before the printing press came to England – Geoffrey Chaucer wrote a book called the *Canterbury Tales,* about a group of travellers who rode from London to a holy shrine in Canterbury Cathedral to pray. In the Middle Ages a lot of people went on pilgrimages like this, and some people went as far as Jerusalem in the Holy Land. The Nun's Priest was one of the pilgrims in Chaucer's book.

Sometimes pilgrims took minstrels to entertain them, but the pilgrims in Chaucer's tale had to make their own amusement. Before setting out, they spent the night in an inn called the Tabard, and the Host of the inn made a suggestion about how they should entertain themselves:

You mean to entertain yourselves by telling stories on the way, I'll be bound; for there's certainly no sense or fun in riding along as dumb as stones; and so..... I'll make up a game that will give you some amusement... Each of you, to make the road seem shorter, shall tell two stories on the journey... Whoever tells his story best is to be given a dinner at the expense of the rest of us......

When you go on holiday, do you sit in the car or on the train as 'dumb as stones'? Explain what Chaucer's pilgrims did to liven up their journey, and then describe some of the things that you do on long journeys to pass the time. What do you do to stop yourself from getting bored on a long journey?

Some of Chaucer's pilgrims were rich and some were poor, some were young and some were old. There were men and women, good people and rogues and they all told different kinds of stories. The Miller was a short, but strong man. Chaucer said that 'there was no door that he couldn't heave off its hinges, or break down by running at it with his head'. He knew all the tricks and ways to steal some of the grain that people brought to his mill, and he always charged a high price to grind the grain. He told a story which made fun of a carpenter. . . .

The Reeve, who was a sort of magistrate, was also a carpenter, and he told a story about a dishonest miller who was paid back for his dishonesty by two students.

There was a Squire, a young man who was training to become a knight. He could compose songs and write music, joust and dance. He loved being in love, . . . like the

ENTERTAINMENT

PROJECT

Wife of Bath, who had married five husbands. She was a merry person who laughed and joked to keep the pilgrims amused. The Scholar spent all of his money on books and education . . . while the Monk loved riding and hunting and thought it was a waste of time reading too many books or working too hard. He told sad tales of people who were ruined by some trouble, and it was after his tale that the Host called for 'something to keep our spirits up.' It was then that the Nun's Priest told his light-hearted story.

Tell the story of Chanticleer and Pertelote in your own words. Don't write it down, but tell it just as one of the pilgrims might have told it. Make sure that the story is clear, and make each different character come alive. Describe how they looked and how they behaved.

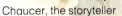
Chaucer, the storyteller

PROJECT

ENTERTAINMENT

In the Market Square

Have you ever acted in a nativity play or seen one performed in your school? It is usually much easier to remember stories if you have seen them acted out, and you probably know the story of the birth of Jesus better than any of the other Bible stories.

In the Middle Ages, while minstrels and Chaucer's pilgrims were travelling the countryside, priests in churches all over the country had to find ways to teach stories in the Bible to the many people who couldn't read. At one time, priests acted out their stories in the church – very simply, without costumes. Then, sometime after 1200, the plays were moved outside the churches to town squares, or other open spaces inside the towns. The market square was a favourite place, because it had always been a centre of entertainment: fairs were held here, travelling players performed here, thieves were put in the stocks, and criminals were hanged while crowds of people watched and music played. And *Mystery plays*, which told Bible stories starting with the Creation and finishing with the death and resurrection of Jesus, were acted out with colourful costumes and lively words!

ENTERTAINMENT PROJECT

The different stories were all acted out in June on Corpus Christi day, which is one of the longest days of the year. The plays often started at sunrise (what time is that in June?) and carried on until sunset. The plays were acted by organisations called *guilds*, which were groups of men who all did the same type of work. There was a Bakers' Guild, an Armourers' Guild, a Gold-Beaters' Guild and many others. Each guild chose a story which was linked with their work. Which of these stories do you think these guilds acted?

1. Shipwrights
2. Tailors
3. Bakers
4. Fishmongers

a. The Last Supper
b. The Feeding of the Five Thousand
c. Joseph and his Coat of Many Colours
d. Noah's Ark

Each play was acted on a horse-drawn wagon, which moved to as many as 16 different 'stations' around the town. The audience stayed at one station and all the plays came to them in turn. You can see from the picture that the wagons had two floors and the stage was on the top one. What was the bottom floor used for? How do you think actors moved from one floor to another? Which play is being acted?

The costumes were sometimes very expensive. One guild spent 35 shillings and 4 pence (£1.77) on a coat and shoes for the actor playing Gabriel, at a time when wages for most of these people would only have been about 3d (1½p) a day. Describe the costumes and the masks that the actors wore.

Write a story set in England today. It is Corpus Christi day, and you are going to see a cycle of Mystery plays acted out by local men. The plays themselves are the very same as they were 600 years ago, but the stations where the plays are acted are different from the one in this picture. Who might you see acting in the plays . . . your milkman, the garage mechanic, computer programmers . . .? What else might have changed?

A modern production of *The Mystery Plays*. Which Bible story is being performed?

PROJECT

ENTERTAINMENT

The Wooden 'O'

This piece of wasteland next to the River Thames will soon be visited by tourists from all over the world. At the moment teams of film directors, actors, scholars and other interested people are planning a project which will involve spending hundreds of thousands of pounds. Why are so many people interested in this patch of land?

To find out, we must go back nearly four hundred years. Let's choose a warm fresh afternoon in 1600, not long before the death of Queen Elizabeth I, and find out what was happening here then.

Crowds of people hurry along the roads, rather like the crowds that you might see outside a football ground on a Saturday afternoon. More people clamber off small boats – they have just come across the river from London. In the distance there is an arena where bull and bear-baiting is held, but this crowd is heading for a tall building nearby . . . the Globe Theatre. A white flag fluttering from the tower of the Globe tells us that a performance is about to start.

The Globe was built in 1599 and was one of the first theatres to be built in England. Before this, actors had usually performed their plays outside or in the courtyards of inns. The Globe was a very popular place – on some days three thousand people might squeeze through the wooden doors, especially if the play that day was by William Shakespeare. Many of Shakespeare's plays were performed here for the first time, and the same plays are performed in many different languages all over the world

The original Globe Theatre and (*above*) a map of the new Globe Theatre site.

today. Some of the performances would really surprise Shakespeare if he could see them!

The project planned for the wasteland next to the Thames is to rebuild the Globe exactly where it was when Shakespeare wrote his plays and as much like the original theatre as possible, so that his plays can be performed as they were when he was still alive.

But how does anyone know what the original theatre was like? It burnt down in 1613. Of course we don't have any

ENTERTAINMENT

PROJECT

photographs, and there aren't even any good clear drawings. Very little evidence has been found: there are a few descriptions by people who visited the Globe or similar theatres, notes giving directions to actors, which help to show us what the stage was like, and Shakespeare himself called the theatre a 'wooden O'. What information does that give us? The illustration on the opposite page shows us what the original Globe looked like.

1. Describe the stage.
2. Today, most stages have 'wings' where actors make their exits and entrances. How did Shakespeare's actors come on and off stage?
3. What sort of scenery did Shakespeare's actors have?

There was always a lot of fidgeting during a performance, and people moved around, talking, fighting, buying beer, oranges and nuts – there was no interval to break up the long performance. The richer people sat in the galleries where they were under cover if it rained. It was cheaper to stand down in front of the stage with the 'groundlings', although from here someone's hat might block the view of the stage! One man who wrote plays at this time said that the audience was like a great beast which the actors had to tame into silence!

Shakespeare wrote funny and sad plays, plays about ghosts and fairies, plays about kings and queens, love stories and stories full of danger, battles and power. Sometimes fireworks were set off during a battle scene to make the scene more realistic and sound effects were made by people off stage. But there was no lighting, no electronic sound effects, no taped music . . .

Draw a picture of the Globe during a performance of one of Shakespeare's plays. Fill up the theatre with a lively audience and try and give a feeling of the fun and enjoyment that everyone had. When the Globe is rebuilt will the audience be very different from Shakespeare's day?

A performance of Shakespeare's *Henry V* in the original Globe Theatre

PROJECT

ENTERTAINMENT

A Story and a Play

If you visit Cornwall, not far from the south-west tip of England, you will find a beautiful theatre carved out of the rocks. Instead of painted scenery, plays performed here have the moon, the sea, perhaps a finger of burning sunset curling round the headland, or even a sea mist as their background. How long has this theatre been there? It looks very like the Greek amphitheatres built over two thousand years ago.

But if we take a closer look, we can see dates carved into the seats, dates of the different plays which have been acted here. The date of the first play to be acted at the Minack is here: *The Tempest 1932*. The theatre wasn't carved out by ancient Greek visitors to Cornwall; pilgrims in the Middle Ages would only have seen bare rocks if they had passed by here, and William Shakespeare would never have imagined that his plays would be performed on these rocks!

Greek amphitheatre at Ancient Epidaurus

ENTERTAINMENT PROJECT

Rowena Cade building her theatre in 1975

actors and the audience. Like the Globe, the Minack is only open for performances during the summer. Why is that? But why can there be evening performances at the Minack, while there were only daytime performances at the Globe?

The audience at the Minack bring something with them in case of rain, which Shakespeare's audience would never have seen! Why can't people hold umbrellas to keep themselves dry? The microphones are hidden under the seats or the stage settings but can you see some evidence of the sound system in the theatre? One recent improvement is a terrace at the top of the cliff where disabled people can sit in wheelchairs. What do people have to make sure that they can hear the play well?

It gets very cold at night so people bring blankets and Thermos flasks with hot drinks. The coffee shop is open in the interval. Why aren't refreshments sold during the performance like they were at the Globe?

In fact the theatre was only begun just over fifty years ago, and building is still going on today. When the Globe was built a skilled team of craftsmen was called in. When most modern theatres are built, a team of building contractors does the work, using cranes, bulldozers and other machinery to help them. But the Minack was built by one woman, Rowena Cade with the help of two men, Billy Rawlings and Charles Thomas Angove. They pushed wheelbarrow loads of sand, stones and earth up the steep cliff sides and they mixed up concrete to build up the seating, carving patterns in the soft concrete to make it look like carved stone.

The first plays were acted with crackly microphones, to try to carry the actors' voices up the cliff side, with a few headlights run on batteries, hurricane lights and wires trailing from Miss Cade's house to bring a weak light to the stage ... and no safety precautions! In 1932, there was no safety barrier between the stage and a steep plunge into the sea!

Fifty years after the first play was acted here, Shakespeare's play *The Tempest* was acted again, but by this time things had become much easier for the

Sometimes there are problems with scenery, because heavy things can't be carried down the cliffs. When a film crew wanted a grand piano, one had to be built on the stage – but it was too light, and a strong gust of wind blew it away!

The Minack is quite different from Shakespeare's open-air theatre but it is also quite different from modern indoor theatres. Make a list of some of the differences between the Globe and the Minack, and then think of some things which are similar. Think about the stage, the seating, the scenery, the type of audience, the lighting and sound, the way people arrived at the theatres.

77

PROJECT

ENTERTAINMENT

A Relaxing Interval

Let's visit the household of a medieval nobleman while he is enjoying his midday meal with his family and guests. Pages have just taken away the basins of scented water and towels, now that everyone has washed their hands, and the meal is ready. There is no hurry. Everyone was awake early and they have been out hunting so they have built up a healthy appetite. Now they want to relax and enjoy themselves. There is plenty of food, including some fresh meat from hunting trips, and between each course minstrels, jugglers and musicians will entertain them.

The younger guests have been warned how to behave. The young girls were reminded that, if they had to share a trencher or a plate, they should leave the best food to the gentlemen, and they shouldn't scratch their dogs or their heads during a meal. No one should search for head lice or fleas, spit on the floor, blow their nose on the tablecloth, or cough or sneeze too loudly while the lord is talking. But not everyone remembers.

Imagine that you are a page serving at the table of this lord. Describe the welcome that is given to the guests. What is the entertainment like? What instruments do the musicians play? What other noises are there in the large hall? Why do you have to be careful where you walk?

ENTERTAINMENT PROJECT

PROJECT

ENTERTAINMENT

The Falcon and the White Hart

A Hunt in the Forest painted by Uccello in the fifteenth century

Where had the lord and lady and their guests been that morning before their meal? Just as people have always enjoyed a good story, people have always enjoyed a bit of excitement in their lives. Long ago, everyone had to learn to hunt if they were to get enough food to eat. But over hundreds of years, hunting changed. By the Middle Ages it had become a sport, for fun and not for survival. One way that this lord and lady entertained their guests was by taking them on a hunting trip on their land. Gamekeepers made sure the land was always well-stocked with game.

To become a sport there had to be rules, and one of the main rules was that only a few people could play. In the Middle Ages all the forest areas of England belonged to the king and so did all the animals that lived in the forest. No one was allowed to hunt without permission from the king. Noblemen were sometimes given permission to hunt some smaller animals in the royal forests, such as badgers, hares, weasels and foxes, but villagers weren't even allowed to hunt hares and rabbits to put in their cooking pots. Poachers risked their lives, as laws against people who were caught hunting in the forest were very harsh.

Of course, people couldn't enjoy the sport of hunting if there weren't the animals to chase, so noblemen who owned large areas of land built deer parks in their own grounds to make sure that there were always deer to hunt. The lord and lady would have been ashamed if they had taken their guests out hunting and all they had found were a few rabbits and some birds.

Most of the people in the hunting party set off on horseback, with dogs, like fox hunters today. Who followed on foot? The dogs were carefully trained, either to drive the deer out of hiding, to attack and kill, or to chase the deer if it managed to escape. There were few hand guns then, so the hunters carried crossbows.

A hunting crossbow

80

ENTERTAINMENT PROJECT

One creature which was more highly prized than hunting dogs was the hawk or falcon. These birds have very sharp eyesight and in the wild they hunt small animals and birds as large as herons. With training they can be taught to bring back their prey to their owner. Why is the falconer wearing thick leather gloves? Why do you think the falconer has to keep a hood on the bird until he wants him to go after another creature? Good hawks were very expensive and some cost more than a good horse. They were so valuable that anyone who found a hawk and didn't return it could be imprisoned for two years and had to pay the price of the bird as well.

Today, a lot of people go fox-hunting for the excitement of the chase. Farmers are pleased to have foxes driven off their land as they are a pest and dangerous to the farm animals. But a lot of people believe that hunting is cruel and that foxes could be controlled more humanely. Talk to your teacher and friends about it.

Make up a story about an exciting event that might have happened at one of these public houses.

81

PROJECT

ENTERTAINMENT

Practising for War

RIOT AT FOOTBALL MATCH – 16 DEAD

When Arsenal hit the sixth goal into the back of the Tottenham net, the Spurs supporters rose in fury. With a chilling battle cry, hundreds of people, wearing their team's colours of blue and white, charged menacingly onto the pitch. A gun shot rang out, and the scorer of the last Arsenal goal lay dead on the ground. Supporters and players fought hand to hand and when the Arsenal supporters came to help their heroes, more shots were heard. When mounted police eventually restored order, it was discovered that 16 people had been killed: 4 players, 10 supporters and 2 policemen.

A football riot

If this had really happened, both football clubs involved might have been banned from ever playing again. Yet football supporters *do* fight and sometimes kill supporters of different teams. Why do you think some people get so violent over just a game?

In the Middle Ages this sort of violence actually did happen at events which started out as 'just a game'. The audience turned up at the big event wearing, not the colours of their favourite football team, but the colours of whichever knight they supported. The event which they came to see was a tournament, a huge pretend battle where everyone fought with real weapons. The tournaments were meant to be friendly practices which were held when there were no wars to be fought and when young noblemen had plenty of energy and nothing much to do. Boys born into rich families knew that they would spend a lot of their life away from home fighting in different wars. They enjoyed taking part in tournaments as a way of training for real battle.

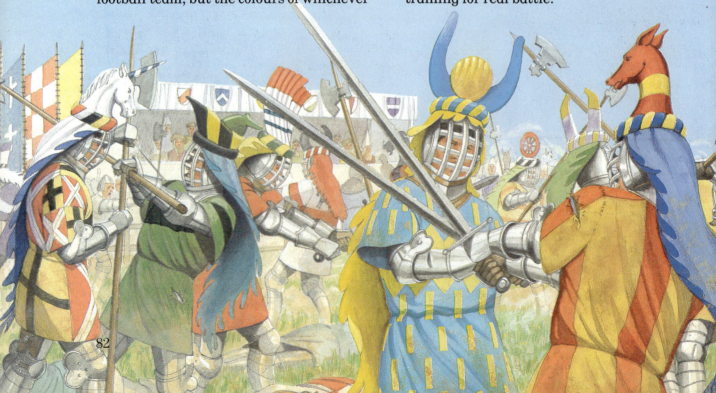

ENTERTAINMENT   PROJECT

Why is this motor-cyclist's helmet better designed than the knight's?

Tournaments were only for the sons of the rich. Good horses were very expensive and so were weapons and armour. Any knight taken prisoner during a tournament had to pay a ransom – a high sum of money – before he could go free. If he didn't pay he might have to give up his horse, his weapons and his armour. Knights who fought well could become very rich as well as being very famous – but they could also lose a lot of money.

The first tournaments often saw thousands of people fighting over miles of countryside. When tempers were lost, spectators joined in the battles to help their heroes and things became very dangerous. Sometimes a lot of people died.

King Edward I tried to stop rioting at tournaments, and he passed a law saying that none of the spectators could carry weapons. After many years, tournaments became more peaceful, and knights came to show off their skills.

1. Why did the knights have to wear helmets? Do you think that they could see clearly? Why was it hard for them to turn their heads?
2. Describe the elaborate armour that the knights wore. Why is the knight being hauled up onto his horse by a pulley? Why did the horses have to be very strong?
3. How could the spectators tell which knights were fighting, even though their faces were covered?

Knights often modelled themselves on King Arthur and his knights of the Round Table – Sir Lancelot, Sir Galahad, Sir Gawain, Sir Kay and others. Try and find out about King Arthur and his knights and their adventures.

The death of King Arthur

83

PROJECT

ENTERTAINMENT

Holding a Tournament

84

ENTERTAINMENT — PROJECT

When tournaments were like wild battles they were very dangerous, but they began to change. They became more like an organised sport with rules and judges to make sure that there was no cheating. Some spectators went to tournaments for the excitement, rather like some football supporters today. Others knew just how skilful the knights were and they kept a record of the points they scored, so that they knew who was 'top of the table' of champions.

The two knights (opposite) are proving their skill in a joust. There were a number of rounds when each knight charged once, and tried to break his lance on his opponent's shield. Extra points were scored if he knocked the other knight off his horse, or if he made a good hit on the crest of his enemy's helmet.

Sometimes the knights fought on foot instead of on horseback. They lost points if they fell onto their knees, and they lost the game if they fell and couldn't get up. Which games today have similar rules?

If the knight was about six foot tall, work out how long his lance was. A coronal was put on the end of the sharp lance to make it less dangerous. What did the coronal look like? Why did the knights have a barrier between them? What skills did a knight need for jousting?

In 1443, Lord Charney held a 'passage of arms', a tournament which lasted for two months. Lord Charney and twelve of his men pretended to be knights defending a mountain pass – in fact it was really a tree – and anyone who wanted to get through had to defeat one of the hosts in a joust. Heralds were sent out to challenge princes, barons, knights and squires from Spain, Italy, France and England, and the prize for defeating one of the champions was five hundred golden crowns – a huge amount of money in those days. More than fifty people took up the challenge and they all brought squires and servants too.

There were also a lot of spectators. Lord Charney opened up three castles to his guests. They all had a room in one, where they kept their armour and weapons. Another castle was like a huge snack bar, where there was food and wine all day. Banquets were held for the guests at the third castle.

Give some of the reasons why a man had to be very rich if he wanted to hold a tournament.

How did the heralds carry the invitations to the guests? Why can someone send out invitations to a party much more easily today?

Imagine that you are a knight living in France. Describe how you get your invitation to Lord Charney's passage of arms. How do you travel to England? Who do you take with you? What is your room in the castle like? Do you defeat Lord Charney in a joust, or does he defeat you?

PROJECT

ENTERTAINMENT

The Sealed Knot

Elaine had checked through her husband's clothes the night before – for such a special day she had to make sure that she hadn't forgotten anything. When Tom was dressed she looked at him. Yes, he looked fine: jacket, breeches, stockings, leather buff coat, cotton collar, sash, baldrick and sword, hat and leather gloves. She knew that her own clothes were fine as she had spent several months carefully sewing them.

After breakfast, Tom checked his sword, picked up his pike and they were ready to go. 'Shall we walk today, my dear?' Tom asked his wife. 'I've already put the camera and the ice-box in the car', Elaine answered. 'I'll drive, if you like!'

Where were Tom and Elaine going in their car, and why were they dressed like a 17th century man and his wife? They belong to a society called *The Sealed Knot* who act out battles which really happened over three hundred years ago, during the English Civil War. But people like Tom and Elaine aren't training for real battles, like the medieval knights used to do. They dress up for the fun and excitement, and to try and feel what it must have been like for the people who really fought in the Civil War battles.

Even though Tom knows that the battle has been organised for fun, and to raise money for charity, he still feels a thrill of fear in his spine when he lines up with the other pikemen to march into battle. But the fear for the Civil War soldier was based on a real danger. The two sides in the battle hated each other and there would be no mercy shown on either side. The Royalist army fought to protect the king, Charles I. They believed that God had made Charles king and God was on their side. The Parliamentarians didn't like the way that Charles ruled the country, and they wanted Parliament to take over the government. They were almost all Puritans (like the Pilgrim Fathers) and they believed that the Royalists were too pleasure-loving and didn't live a religious, God-fearing life. The Parliamentarians believed that God was on *their* side.

Charles I

Pikes of the seventeenth century

This battle (right) was fought in 1984, but you can almost imagine that you are stepping back to the Battle of Marston Moor which was fought in 1644. The clothes are the same as the Royalist and Parliamentarian soldiers wore. The battle is fought with weapons like the ones used in 1644. But there are some signs of the twentieth century. Can you find them?

86

ENTERTAINMENT PROJECT

Some of the foot soldiers couldn't afford the real uniform, but they wore a coloured sash to show whether they were Royalist or Parliamentarian.

In the Royalist army, the foot soldiers were the ordinary villagers, while the cavalry (who fought on horseback) were usually the rich landowners. How can you tell that this is true from the picture? What can you see in the picture which shows us that the Parliamentarians were religious men?

The Royalist pikemen often formed a 'hedgehog' to try to stop the cavalry charge by the enemy. How do you think they did this? The pikes that were really used in the Civil War were wooden, with steel points, but in this friendly battle they are just made of wood.

The wives and daughters of the soldiers followed the progress of the battle and they acted as nurses for the wounded soldiers. The armies did have surgeons but you can see that it was very difficult for them to do anything for the injured until

Plan of the Battle of Naseby, 1645, another Civil War victory for the Parliamentarians, led by Oliver Cromwell

after the battle. Imagine that you were an army surgeon in 1644. Describe what it was like working on the battlefield. What was the noise like? What could you do to help the injured? Describe the death carts. Who did you have to help you? Describe how you had to drive away scavengers – the men and women who came and stole any valuables that they could find from the dead bodies.

'The Sealed Knot' re-enact the battle of Marston Moor

PROJECT

ENTERTAINMENT

Holy Days – Fasting and Football

Today most people remember Shrove Tuesday as Pancake Day. They might eat pancakes for tea, but they still go to work or school. Until quite recently, it was remembered by everyone as the day before the Christian festival of Lent began. It was a Holy day, when the Pancake Bell rang in the villages to remind everyone to go to church to confess their sins before Lent began. But as well as being a *Holy day* it was also a *holiday*. During Lent, everyone was expected to fast and eat simple food, so on Shrove Tuesday everyone made pancakes and had a feast to use up the rich food in their larders. How did the poor people who had empty larders manage to make pancakes?

In many villages, Shrove Tuesday was one of the best days of the year, when everyone had a holiday and could enjoy themselves. One of the most popular Shrovetide games was football, but it was very different from the game that you can play or watch today. In 1314, King Edward I tried to ban the game because it was so dangerous, but the ban didn't work, as you know. In 1584, one man described football as a 'murdering business'. He said it was so dangerous for the players that 'sometimes their necks are broken, sometimes their backs, sometimes their legs, sometimes their arms . . .'

There weren't proper teams and sometimes whole villages joined in the game, while the goals could be miles apart across streams and ditches. Sam Armitage loved the excitement of the game, but John Partridge called it 'mob football' and wanted it banned. With a friend, argue the case for and against football, as it used to be played. One of you give Sam's point of view, and one of you argue John's case.

ENTERTAINMENT | PROJECT

Bear-baiting in 1821

Cock-fighting in the early nineteenth century

Then wander round the village and describe some of the other games that were popular at Shrovetide. Bear-baiting and cock-fighting were popular sports all year round until the 19th century. Do you think cock-fighting and bear-baiting were cruel? Why do you think people enjoyed watching them? Was it a good idea to ban them?

Early football match – over 400 years ago

PROJECT

ENTERTAINMENT

Remember, Remember, the Fifth of November...

Bonfire and fireworks and (*right*) The Yeomen of the Guard searching the Houses of Parliament

Why do both of these things happen every year on the same day, November 5th? Why are the Houses of Parliament searched by men wearing 17th century clothes – only on this one day? And why do we light bonfires and burn a guy – only on this one day? People in France don't celebrate November 5th, nor do the Dutch or the Americans. So what is it that we should be remembering?

You probably all know that a man called Guy Fawkes tried to blow up the Houses of Parliament and failed. That was in 1605. But why did he want to kill the king and the Members of Parliament? Guy Fawkes and the other men involved in the plot were all Catholics. King James I and the men who helped him to run the country were all Anglicans. In your class there are probably children of different religions, who all worship in different places and have different customs, but who are all friends.

But people haven't always been able to worship where and how they want. When Guy Fawkes and his friends planned the Gunpowder Plot, there was only one religion in England that people could practise safely, and that was the religion of the king. Until the sixteenth century the main religion in England was Catholicism, but Henry VIII refused to accept the authority of the Pope. He made himself head of the Church in England, and many people followed him. Henry's daughter, Mary, stayed a Catholic and when she became queen in 1553, she tried to force a lot of people to accept the Pope's authority. Some people who refused were burnt at the stake. This made people hate and fear the Roman Catholics. Under Queen Elizabeth I, and King James I, Catholics weren't allowed to hold good jobs. And they weren't even allowed to practise their religion freely.

Henry VIII   Mary I   James I of England

Guy Fawkes and the other men involved in the plot hid in a room underneath the place where James I and his ministers were going to meet on November 5th, 1605. They took gunpowder, which was the common explosive used in battles, and they plotted to blow up the men who made laws against Catholics. Then the Catholics would take over the running of the country themselves. James heard rumours of the plot and ordered a search to be made. Guy Fawkes was caught with the gunpowder ... and James I ordered November 5th to be a public holiday for everyone, to celebrate how the government of England had been saved!

People held celebrations in November with bonfires and feasting for hundreds of years before Guy Fawkes was born. Before the Romans came to England, the Celtic

ENTERTAINMENT

PROJECT

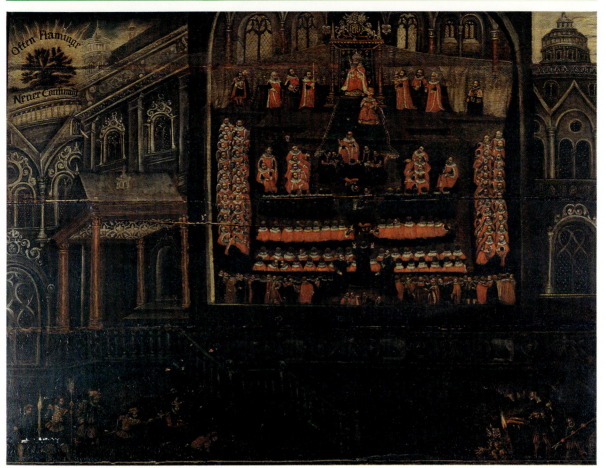

The Gunpowder Plot, 1605, a painting showing James I and his ministers, with Guy Fawkes and his men hiding under the Houses of Parliament

people killed some of their cows in November because there wasn't enough grass to feed them through the winter. Most of the meat was salted to last the winter, but some was eaten at a big feast, and a bonfire was built to frighten evil spirits away from the earth, so that next year's crops would grow well.

A Celtic feast, 2,000 years ago

One of the many Bonfire Society groups that celebrate major events in Lewes' history every year, in November

Describe some of the differences between the Celtic bonfire night and the big celebrations that are held in Lewes in Sussex now. How many things *haven't* changed?

Write a report for a London newspaper for November 6th, 1605. You can be either an Anglican reporter writing about the lucky failure of the Gunpowder Plot, or a Catholic reporter. How are the Catholic and Anglican reports different?

PROJECT

ENTERTAINMENT
All the Fun of the Fair

Southwark Fair, London, in the eighteenth century

All over the country, adults and children used to have a day off work or a holiday from school so that they could join in the fun on Shrove Tuesday and Guy Fawkes Day. In the same way everyone stopped work when the fair came to their town. What do you like to do at the fair? In the Middle Ages you would have seen the travelling players at the fair, but most of the stalls were more like market stalls than fairground booths that you see today. Merchants came from foreign countries with beautiful things to sell, things that couldn't normally be found in England. They brought silks, furs, spices and precious jewels and in return they took woollen cloth made in England and tin from the English mines. Find out if there is a fair in your town or a town nearby. If there is, find out how old it is and how it has changed over the years.

In Oxford, a huge fair is held every September in a busy street called St. Giles. The traffic is stopped on the days of the fair. It is hard to believe that it could be held there when you see the buses and cars on a normal day.

Study the three pictures of street fairs on this page. How are they different and which would you rather go to?

Oxford's St. Giles' fair is quite young compared with other fairs that have been held on the same spot since the Middle Ages. But people have been having fun on this street for almost two hundred years. Most country people had a few extra pennies in their pockets in September after they had worked hard bringing in the harvest, and even in the towns there was more work than usual in the summer so there was more money to spend. Thousands of people came in to Oxford from the villages, on carriers' carts, by pony and trap, on foot, or on the special cheap excursion trains.

St Giles' fair, Oxford, in the nineteenth century and as it looks today

ENTERTAINMENT PROJECT

A nineteenth-century steam-driven roundabout

Like the medieval fairs, there were market stalls where people could buy presents or 'fairings' – gingerbread and dolls for the children, tobacco, snuff and bright paintings. Young couples could buy all sorts of things for their homes – saucepans, baking tins, brooms, baskets, material and ribbons. Quack doctors promised to cure toothaches, warts and pimples with a magic liquid, and fortune tellers promised to tell the future to anyone who would slip them some money. Recruiting sergeants promised young farm workers a better life if they joined the army, and policemen promised something worse if young boys didn't behave themselves.

The fair saw all kinds of changes. Describe how the first roundabouts worked. In the 1860s steam-driven roundabouts came to the fair. How different did they look?

Until the 1850s the fair was a gloomy place at night and pickpockets could work safely in the dark. How did the fair people light their stalls? In 1862 one sweet stall drew crowds because of its new form of gas lighting, and in 1882, crowds of people stared as they saw the new bright electric lights for the first time.

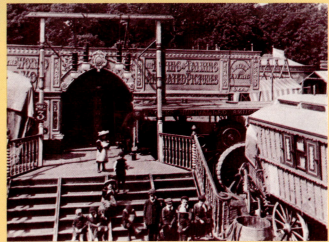

A bioscope 'moving picture show' at a fair in 1907

Large crowds were drawn to the booth that showed the moving pictures or bioscope. People herded into a dark tent, where they stood patiently while someone battled with a projector and a tangled film until at last a flickering, black and white moving picture appeared on the screen. Then everyone gasped in wonder as stories of crimes and wars, love stories and tales from Shakespeare passed before their eyes.

Do you have a day off school when the fair comes to town? Imagine that you were a child in 1850 and describe what it was like to go to the fair. What was it like in the evening before there was gas or electric lighting? Go and visit some of the boothes that you can see in the picture of the fair. Taste the different food and buy some fairings to take home with you.

93

PROJECT

ENTERTAINMENT

Talking Pictures

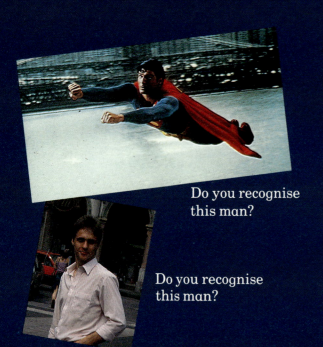

Do you recognise this man?

Do you recognise this man?

Why will most people say yes to the first question and only a few will say yes to the second question?

Make a list of some of the ways in which a person can become famous today with some examples. Would your list have been very different a hundred years ago? The most familiar face then was the queen's face. But when cinemas became popular in the 1920s the same faces could be seen all over the country on the same night.

The first films in England were very short. This poster advertised some of the films that people could see in 1897 in one of the first British cinemas. The pictures may not look particularly exciting to us, because we are so used to moving pictures.

But to early cinema goers, the very fact that they could watch the rabbit appear from the conjurer's hat, or a man dive into a pool, was almost a miracle.

It wasn't long before full length films were made, more like the ones we watch today – except for one very important thing. The early films had no sound. The story had to be acted very clearly, often in a very exaggerated manner. Sometimes some words were printed on the screen to explain what was happening and music was played on a piano or organ to help build up a good atmosphere in the cinema. Try making up a story which you can tell in pictures, like in a comic. But don't use any words. It isn't easy! The first 'talking' pictures in the late 1920s opened up great possibilities.

One of the first cinema advertisements in Britain in 1897

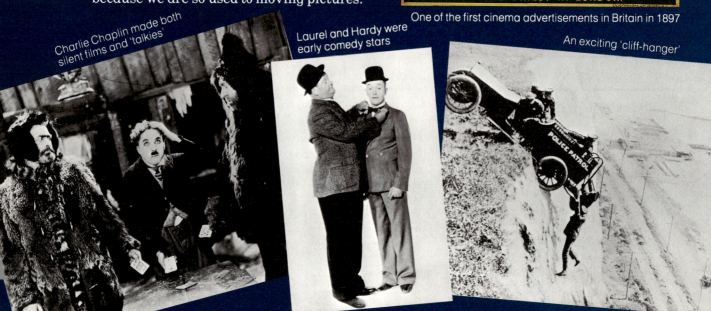

Charlie Chaplin made both silent films and 'talkies'

Laurel and Hardy were early comedy stars

An exciting 'cliff-hanger'

ENTERTAINMENT PROJECT

But this didn't mean that the silent movies were dull! As film makers became more skilled, films became longer and more elaborate. Cowboy films and adventure films were very popular and must have seemed very real to the audience. One visitor to an American cinema in 1914 fired his gun at the screen when he thought that the hero was going to be hung. The audience would cheer actions by the heroes and boo the villains.

Going to the cinema was much more popular in the days of the silent movies and the early 'talkies' than it is today. For nearly 60 years cinema was the most popular form of entertainment for children and adults before television took over in the 1960s. Many people would go to the 'pictures' or the 'flicks' twice a week, paying 3d (1½p) or 6d (2½p) for their ticket, and there were special performances for children on Saturdays. Like television serials today, the Saturday films would often end on a 'cliff-hanger' so that the children would come back next week to see how the hero and heroine managed to escape.

For many people, a visit to the cinema was a marvellous escape from dull humdrum lives. The names of the cinemas were lavish and exotic: there were picture palaces and temples called the Grand, the Trocadero, the Majestic, the World's Window, Roxy, the Rialto, the Empress. Many of the cinemas looked as exotic as they sounded. How do these names compare with the names of your nearest cinemas?

One of the earliest English films was called 'Rescued by Rover' (1905). It cost less than £8 to make. Do you know how much it cost to make 'Superman', or any other of today's films? See if you can find out. In 1909 one film company paid their actors 7s 6d (37½p) a day if they had a leading part and 5s (25p) a day for a smaller part. But as the cinema became more popular, the actors began to realise their value to the film makers. By 1916, Charlie Chaplin could ask $10,000 a week, plus a starting bonus of $150,000. Now top film stars are paid $4 or $5 million dollars for acting in one film.

But cinema wasn't simply entertainment and fun. Imagine how newsreel of action on the Western Front during the First World War must have affected the parents and sisters of the men fighting so far away.

Newsreel from the 1914-18 war

What do you think William the Conqueror would have said if you had been transported back to 1066 with a camera in your hand?

What would the Pilgrim Fathers have said if they could have seen a travel film about the New World before they left Plymouth harbour? What would Charlie Chaplin have said if he had seen colour films with soundtracks playing in most homes? What might happen in the world of film and entertainment to surprise us in the next few years?

E.T.

An early cinema

Inside an early cinema

INDEX

A
actors 47, 94–95
advertisements 8–9, 10–11, 12–13, 19, 94
America 26, 36, 43, 95
anaesthetics 57, 62
anatomy 58–59
antiseptics 61, 63
archaeologist 4, 6, 8, 18
Ascension Day 15, 17
Australia 26, 53

B
babies 54, 57, 62
Bampton, Oxon 45, 47, 51
barber-surgeons 57
baths 12–13
Battle of Marston Moor 86
Battle of Naseby 87
Battle of Worcester 14
bear-baiting 89
Bible 24, 47, 72–73
bioscope 93
Black Death 15, 55
books 46, 48–49
Boyes Staith, Yorks 17
brick making 24–25, 32
brick tax 25
Burry Man 15

C
Cade, Rowena 77
Cambridge University 23
Canada 26
canals 23
Canterbury Tales 68–69
Caxton, William 48
Charles I, King 14, 86–87
Charles II, King 14, 15
Charney, Lord 85
Chaucer, Geoffrey 70–71, 72
cholera 55
cinemas 94–95
Civil War 86–87
clothes dryer 11, 19
coal 13
cock fighting 89
Columbus, Christopher 36–37, 45
coronal 85
Corpus Christi 73
Cucklet Delf 14–15

D
dentist 57
doctor 56, 58, 60

E
Edward VII, King 13
Egypt 24
Elizabeth I, Queen 27, 74
Exeter & Bridgewater canal 22–23
explorers 34–35, 36–37
Eyam 14–15

F
fairs 92–93
falconer 81
Fawkes, Guy 90–91, 92
films 94–95
First World War 5, 9, 12, 95
football match 82, 88–89
fox hunting 81
France 5, 14, 25

G
gas lighting 11, 93
George III, King 25
germs 54
Globe Theatre 74–75, 77
gramophone 4–5
Gunpowder Plot 90–91

H
Harrod's Store 10–11
Henry VI, King 23
Henry VII, King 17
herbal medicine 56
Hill, Rowland 29
Holy days 88
hospitals 60–61
hunting 80–81

I
Indians, American 37, 41
Iron Age 7

J
Jenner, Edward 59, 63

K
Kelly's Directory 30–31, 33
King's College, Cambridge 23
King's Messenger 28
knights 83, 84–85

L
Lent 88
Lister, Joseph 61
Little Moreton Hall 21
Lower Brockhampton Manor House 20–21, 23

M
Magdalen College, Oxford 17
Malcolm III, King 15
manor house (construction) 20–21
maps 34, 42, 45
Mary I, Queen 23
May morning 17
Mayflower, The 39, 40, 43, 53
medicine 56
Middle Ages 44, 46, 51, 52, 58, 72, 80
Minack Theatre, Cornwall 76–77
minstrels 66–67, 78–79
monks 46
Mystery plays 73

N
newspapers 8
news 50, 53, 95
Nightingale, Florence 60

O
Oak Apple Day 14
oil lighting 11, 19
operating theatre 61
Oxford 17, 92

P
Parliamentarians 86–87
Penny Hedge 17
penny post 28
Pilgrims 38–39, 40–41, 43, 53, 70–71, 72, 95
plague 14, 55, 58
Plymouth 31
Pope, The 90
Post House 27, 28
post, mail 26, 28–29, 33
Post Office 29, 33
pots 6–7
printing 48–49

Q
Q.E.2 39

R
railways 23, 29, 51
Raleigh, Sir Walter 36–37
Roche Abbey 23
Roman baths 25
Roman Catholics 90
Romans 7, 18, 25, 35
Royalists 86–87
Royal Mail 26–27, 50

S
St. Giles' Fair, Oxford 92
Saxons 7, 18, 35
Scotland 15
Sealed Knot 86–87
settlers 35, 37, 42
sea travel 39
Shakespear, William 74–75, 76–77, 93
Shrove Tuesday 88, 92
smallpox 59
South Queensferry 15
Spain 27
stamps 29
steam engine 12
stone 23, 45
Stone Age 7, 18
storytelling 66
surgeon 57, 63

T
taxes 25
telephone 9, 13
Thanksgiving feast 41
thatched roofs 21
theatre 65, 73, 74–75, 76–77

Tichborne Dole 16–17
Tichborne, Sir Roger 16
Tissington 15
tournaments 82–83, 84

U
underground train 29

V
vaccinations 59
Victoria, Queen 9, 57
Vikings 35
Virginia (USA) 37
voyages 36, 38–39

W
war 5, 9, 12, 95
washing machines 11, 19
well blessing 15
Whitby, Abbot of 17
William the Conqueror 15, 35, 50, 95

X
X-rays 59

A HISTORY OF AFRICA

Robin Walker

FRANKLIN WATTS
LONDON·SYDNEY

First published in Great Britain in 2024 by Hodder & Stoughton
Copyright © Hodder & Stoughton Limited, 2024
All rights reserved.

Editor: Julia Bird
Designer: Emma DeBanks
Consultant: Dr Onyeka Nubia, historian

Picture credits: AKG Images; 25r; André Held 21c; Andrea-Jemolo 24t; Pictures from History 7b.
Alamy: Afripics F cover tcr; Album18b; AP 38b; Paolo Certo F cover tcl; Chronicle 23t, 32t; CPA Media Pte Ltd 21b; Ian Dagnall Computing 17b, 20; Ran Dembo 31b; Everett Collection 35t; Horst Friedrichs 19b;Greatstock 5t; Peter Horree 13b; De Luan 10; PA Images 34r; Christopher Scott 22; Mike P Shepherd 7t; SJArt 29; The Print Collector 32b; UPI 39b;
World History Archive 12t, 17; Xinhua 37b, 42. Florida Center for Instructional Technology/©2004-2023 27t.
Library of Congress, USA/Frances Benjamin Johnston 37t.
Magnum: Ernest Cole 33.
Shutterstock: Africulture 20; Anabela88 F cover c; Anelena 6t; AlexAnton 44cr; Thomas Bartelds 43t; Bist 9b; cowardlion 45; Maciej Czekajewski 4t; Daily Travel Photos 24b; Deyan Denchev F cover tc; Rudi Ernst 15t; Everett Collection 28b, 36b; Givaga 8; Homo Cosmicos15b, 26b; Iulius background grids; Jezper f cover bcr; Vladislav T Jirousek 14b; Aleksandar Kamasi 11t; Carlo Kaminski 43b; Kavram f cover bc; Ekaterina Khudina 18t; Trevor Kittelty 19t; kowition 4b; Felix Lipov 6b; Macrowildlife 23b; gustavo mellossa 37c; Mitz f cover bl; Jaroslav Moravcik 16; Jean du Plessis 41b; Torsten Pursche 31t; Matyas Rehak 12b; Mark Reinstein 35b, 39c; Sculpies f cover br; Joseph Sohm f cover bcl;Rich T Photo f cover tr; Dietmar Temps 40; Massimo Todaro 41t; Alena Vesey 44rc; Vladimir Wrangel 11b; Xamnesiacx84 f cover tl;Zampe238 13t.
Daniel Orme, W. Denton, Olaudah Equiano (Gustavus Vassa) 1789, from "The Interesting Narrative of the Life of Olaudah Equiano or Gustavus Vassa, the African" Published by G. Vassa, London, March 1789: 8t.
Wikimedia: Ismoon/CCA SA 4.0 International 14t; PBA Lille/CCA SA 4.0 International;
Werner Ustort/ CCA-SA 2.0 Generic; Henry Sylvester Williams/PD 34bl.
Every effort has been made to clear copyright. Should there be any inadvertent omission,
please apply to the publisher for rectification.

Printed in Dubai
HB ISBN: 978 1 4451 8733 4
PB ISBN: 978 1 4451 8732 7

An Hachette UK Company
www.hachette.co.uk
www.hachettechildrens.co.uk
Franklin Watts
An imprint of Hachette Children's Group
Part of Hodder and Stoughton
Carmelite House
50 Victoria Embankment
London EC4Y 0DZ

The websites (URLs) included in this book were valid at the time of going to press. However, it is possible that the contents or addresses may have changed since the publication of this book. No responsibility for any such changes can be accepted by either the author or the Publisher.

INTRODUCTION

The history of Africa is rich and varied, and far too much to be covered in one book. This book is just an introduction, designed to be accessible for young readers and using a select group of simplified examples. *A History of Africa* is not intended to end a reader's research of Africa, but to begin it. To understand Africa is to explore the connections this continent has with the world. African history is an essential part of world history and we should all know about and understand it. This book will start readers on their journey.

Dr. O.Nubia

CONTENTS

African history 4	Resistance 28
From prehistory to kingdoms 6	In focus: African religions 30
Ancient Egypt 8	Colonialism 32
Egypt invaded 10	Independence for Africa 34
Kush 12	In focus: African culture abroad ... 36
Ethiopia 14	After independence 38
In focus: Famous African rulers 16	Africa today – challenges 40
West African empires 18	Africa today – successes 42
The Nigeria region 20	Teaching African history 45
Great Zimbabwe and Munhumutapa ... 22	Timeline, glossary and further information ... 46
In focus: Treasures of Africa 24	Index 48
The enslaved 26	

AFRICAN HISTORY

Savannah, or grassland, spreads across half of Africa's landscape.

The huge continent of Africa has a very important place in world history. It is the place where the first humans evolved, millions of years ago.

Africa is Earth's second largest continent – only Asia is bigger.

Today, Africa is home to more than a billion people. It covers over 20 per cent of the Earth's surface, stretching over 8,000 km from north to south. Its landscape ranges from desert to dense rainforest and white beaches. Its history is long, rich and complex, taking in migrations, foreign invasions and hard-fought independence.

NAMING AFRICA
There are different theories as to how Africa got its name. It may have been named after the Roman name for an African tribe, the 'Afri', for the Greek word 'a-phrike', meaning 'without cold', or for the Latin word for sunny, 'aprica'.

4

WHAT IS AFRICAN HISTORY?

History is the record of what humans have done to shape the world around them. It is found in written documents and in remains found or excavated (dug up) by archaeologists. It can also be discovered through myths, stories and legends. To write African history, historians interpret the past by examining these different pieces of evidence and making decisions about what is likely to have happened.

Rock art and tools reveal that humans lived in Wonderwerk Cave in South Africa nearly two million years ago.

WHY SHOULD YOU BE INTERESTED IN AFRICAN HISTORY?

Humans are of African origin. People from all over the world, if they could trace their family history, would end up in Africa. Archaeologists have discovered the oldest known skeletons of modern humans in Ethiopia. Scientists dated those remains and found they were 195,000 years old. Earlier forms of humans were also discovered in Africa, some of them dating back to five million years ago.

THE FIRST MIGRATIONS

People are believed to have started migrating north out of Africa and into Asia around two million years ago. Much more recently, modern humans moved from Africa towards the Middle East around 60–90,000 years ago, from there spreading out and settling around the world. These first travellers would have had rich, dark skin. As populations mixed, skin tones became lighter in later generations.

A reconstruction of Cheddar Man, a 10,000-year-old skeleton found at Cheddar Gorge in England. He has dark skin – a hint at his African heritage.

5

FROM PREHISTORY TO KINGDOMS

It was in Africa that some of the first mines were dug, tens of thousands of years ago. Prehistoric Africans also showed knowledge of maths, astronomy and animal farming. These achievements laid the basis for one of the world's first kingdoms – Ta-Seti.

ANCIENT MINING

In 1964 an ancient mine was found in the mountains of Bomvu Ridge, Eswatini. Archaeologists uncovered tunnels, tools and mine entrances. In total, they found 300,000 artefacts, including thousands of stone tools. The site is believed to date back 43,200 years, making it likely to be the oldest mine in the world. The miners dug for a mineral called specularite, which they may have used as a dye.

Specularite is often silvery or grey as it contains lots of iron ore.

Ngwenya Mine, on the site of the ancient mine on Bomvu Ridge, was still in use until 2014.

CAVE CRAFT
Later peoples extracted red ochre (haematite) from the mine, which they used to create cave paintings.

EARLY ACHIEVEMENTS

In the Lebombo Mountains between South Africa, Mozambique and Eswatini, archaeologists have found a piece of mathematical evidence, thought to be around 37,000 years old. It is a baboon leg bone, carved with 29 notches and 30 spaces. It was probably used as a calendar, showing the average length of a lunar month. In the Lukenya Hill district in Kenya, people domesticated cattle 15,000 years ago. Archaeologists have found teeth and bones spread over a small area, suggesting that humans controlled the movement of the cattle.

In Nabta Playa in Egypt, archaeologists have found a stone circle known as the Calendar Circle. It was built around 8,000 years ago and its stones are believed to line up with the stars to track the changing seasons.

Some of the stones of the Calendar Circle are aligned to the three stars of the constellation, Orion's Belt.

THE FIRST KINGDOM

In 1962, archaeologists discovered the tombs of a dynasty of between nine and 11 pharaohs of Nubia at Qustul, near the modern Egyptian-Sudanese border. Their kingdom was called Ta-Seti, meaning 'land of the bow' and it rose from around 3,800 BCE. The tombs contained 5,000 artefacts of Ta-Seti. Most were locally made, but others were acquired by trade with their neighbours. Boats appear on the art and show how they travelled to trade. Pottery helped the archaeologists to date the site by comparing it to ancient Egyptian pottery. They found that the first of the Nubian pharaohs ruled two or three hundred years before the first pharaoh of Egypt.

The Qustul censer is a Nubian incense burner. Made of limestone, it is believed to date from around 3200 BCE.

ANCIENT EGYPT

Every year, millions of tourists visit Egypt to see its pyramids, temples and statues. The story of ancient Egypt (then known as Kemet) is of the rise and fall of 30 ruling families called dynasties who held power for thousands of years.

THE AGE OF PYRAMIDS

Dynasty 1 to Dynasty 6 is known as the Old Kingdom Period of ancient Egypt, and dates from around 3100–2181 BCE. The greatest achievements of its 50 rulers were the building of the Great Pyramids and the Sphinx. This period is remembered as one of great prosperity, during which Egypt became an urban (city-based) civilisation. Cities, towns and ports grew up, dotted along the River Nile.

SECRETS OF THE SPHINX

The Great Sphinx of Giza is one of the oldest known colossal statues. Carved in the shape of a lion, it has the head of an Egyptian pharaoh. Most historians think that a pharaoh from Dynasty 4, King Khafre, ordered it to be built in around 2500 BCE but no one knows for sure. Its missing nose also remains a mystery!

The Great Sphinx sits in front of the Pyramid of Khafre in Giza, near Egypt's capital, Cairo.

MIDDLE KINGDOM EGYPT

The families of Dynasty 11 and 12 ruled during the Middle Kingdom Period, which stretched from around 2040 to 1786 BCE. The Middle Kingdom rulers spent less on grand monuments and more on practical things. They excavated wells and reservoirs, built roads and encouraged trade. Senwosret II, the fourth ruler of Dynasty 12, commissioned the city of Kahun to be built for workers constructing a nearby pyramid. It was a planned city with a grid of straight roads.

NEW KINGDOM EGYPT

Dating from around 1560 to 1080 BCE, Dynasties 18 to 20 ruled over Egypt's New Kingdom Period. The greatest achievement of its 31 rulers was the construction of the majestic temple complexes of Karnak and Luxor. During the time of Amenhotep III, Egypt enjoyed prosperity. The capital city of Waset grew to have a population of one million people, spread over 15 square kilometres on both sides of the Nile.

Under the rule of Senwosret II, Egypt was peaceful and prosperous.

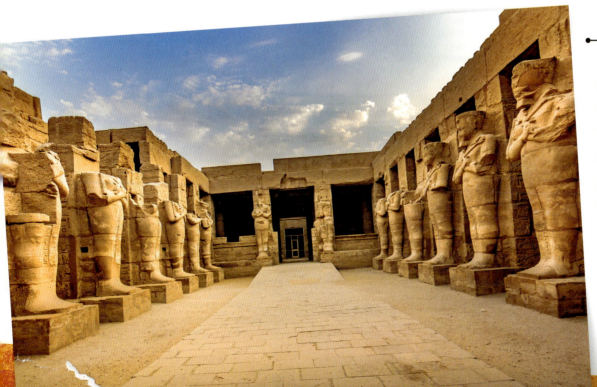

The Valley of the Kings is found on the west bank of the Nile, near Luxor. Many New Kingdom pharaohs were buried here.

EGYPT INVADED

The population of ancient Egypt was transformed over time, as invaders from the Middle East and southern Europe displaced but also mingled with the Egyptian people.

PERSIAN RULE

In 525 BCE the Persians invaded and conquered Egypt from Persia (modern-day Iran) in the Middle East. Egypt became part of the Persian Empire. The Persians held power over Egypt on and off until 332 BCE. Throughout this period, indigenous kings fought back and attempted to break free from Persian rule.

HERODOTUS

The Persian conquerors allowed Greek scholars to enter Egypt. Among them was Herodotus (c.484–425 BCE), a historian who wrote an account of his time in Egypt. It gives us valuable information about daily life there.

Cambyses II, king of the Persian Empire, enters the Egyptian city of Memphis in 525 BCE.

THE GREEKS TAKE OVER

The ancient Greeks took Egypt from Persia in 332 BCE, led by Alexander the Great. Some Egyptians saw him as a saviour who defeated the Persians and ended their cruelty. Alexander founded a city on the Mediterranean coast of Egypt called 'Alexandria'. It became the intellectual capital of the Greek Empire. Eventually, a Greek general was crowned Pharaoh Ptolemy I in around 305 BCE.

ROMAN RULE

Cleopatra VII was the last ruler of the Greek dynasty. Of Greek and African heritage, she lived when the Romans were a rising power in the Mediterranean region. Under Julius Caesar, the Romans conquered Egypt in 48 BCE. However, Cleopatra persuaded Julius Caesar and his successor, Mark Anthony, to share power with her. In 30 BCE, Octavius, a Roman rival, deposed Cleopatra and put Egypt under direct rule. The Romans ruled North Africa for the next 600 years. During their reign, Christianity became an important part of Egyptian culture.

ARAB RULERS

In turn, people from Arabia conquered Egypt from the Middle East in CE 639. By CE 708 they had seized the whole of North Africa. They are still the ruling population of Egypt today.

A statue of Alexander the Great in Thessaloniki, Greece.

Cleopatra and her son, Caesarion (centre). Caesarion's father was Julius Caesar.

KUSH

Over the years, the ancient Nile kingdom of Kush became a powerful rival to its neighbour, Egypt. Its culture centred on the cities of Kerma, Napata and Meroë.

GROWING POWER

Kush began as a kingdom, but later grew into an empire. Located in today's Sudan, Kerma was its capital city and flourished from around 2400 BCE. Kush's soldiers, armed with bows and arrows, were famous for their skills in warfare. The Egyptians built huge castles to keep them at bay. However, Kush seized the Sai kingdom to the north, and later took over the whole region up to the Egyptian border. They controlled gold mines and trade routes and had the finest ceramics industry in the ancient world.

A stone figurine of King Taharqo, one of Kush's greatest rulers.

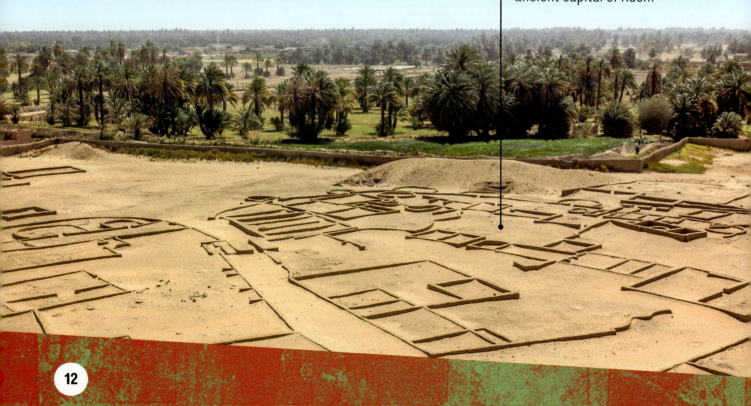

The archaeological site at Kerma, ancient capital of Kush.

These Kushite pyramids, found near Meroë, are believed to date back to the 3rd or 4th century BCE.

RISE AND FALL

Kush fell under Egypt's control during the New Kingdom period, but flourished again between 860 BCE and CE 350. At least 223 pyramids were built during this period, far more than in neighbouring Egypt. From their new capital in Napata, Kush conquered Egypt and parts of the Middle East. Taharqo was its greatest ruler. King from 690 to 664 BCE, he called himself the Emperor of the World, and conquered from land from North Africa as far as Spain. However, the Assyrians from the Middle East fought back. They seized Egypt from Kush in CE 663 and the Kushite Empire collapsed.

CHRISTIAN KINGDOMS

The Sudan region became powerful again between the 4th and 15th centuries CE. Two Christian kingdoms flourished: Makuria and Alwa. Among their ruins, archaeologists have discovered walled towns and cities featuring housing complexes with running water and water heating systems, toilets and glass windows.

This stone is carved with the Meroïtic script.

MEROË

Meroë became the new capital of Kush from 590 BCE. From the fourth century CE, the Kushites invented a new script called Meroïtic, which combines letters and picture symbols called hieroglyphs.

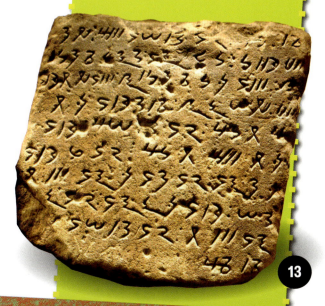

ETHIOPIA

Ethiopia has many thousands of years of rich history. Tourists flock to see the obelisks in Axum, the underground churches of Lalibela and famous castles in Gondar.

The famous gold coin proclaiming Axum's conversion to Christianity.

THE AXUMITE EMPIRE

A powerful trading empire, Axum was found where the countries of Ethiopia and Eritrea are today. At its height, between 300–600 CE, many considered Axum to be the third most powerful empire in the world after Persia and Rome. Twenty of its rulers appear on golden and silver coins minted in the capital city Axum, among the first coins to be made in Africa.

Adorning Axum are seven giant stone pillars called obelisks, carved between 300 BCE and 300 CE. The largest obelisk, now fallen, was then the largest such structure in the world.

In 330 CE, thanks to its links to Syria, Axum adopted Christianity as the state religion. King Ezana issued coins with the Christian cross on them that said: "May the country be satisfied!"

The ancient obelisks of Axum are now a UNESCO World Heritage Site.

BACK TO AFRICA
One obelisk was seized by Italian soldiers in 1937 during a war and taken to Italy as a trophy. It was returned to Axum and re-erected in 2008.

RISING FROM THE GROUND

Lalibela became the new capital of the Ethiopian Empire, which replaced the Axumite Empire, during the 12th century CE. It is famous for its 11 Christian churches, built between 1180 and 1220 during the reign of King Lalibela. While churches in Europe rose to the sky, the churches here were dug out of the ground and connected to each other by a series of tunnels and passages.

THE CAMELOT OF AFRICA

In the 1700s, Gondar became the new capital of the Ethiopian Empire. Founded by Emperor Fasilides in 1635, it had schools, churches, gardens, pools and zoos and became known as 'the Camelot of Africa' because of the 20 or so castles built there. However, much of this precious heritage would later be lost. The British invaded Ethiopia in 1868 and stole priceless artefacts: precious books, church art and intricate royal crowns.

The Church of Saint George in Lalibela.

The site of Fasilides' castles in Gondar, Ethiopia.

IN FOCUS

FAMOUS AFRICAN RULERS

African history is full of famous kings and queens. Some are remembered for their great deeds, others for their mysterious deaths.

TUTANKHAMEN, THE BOY KING

Tutankhamen was the 12th ruler of Egypt's Dynasty 18. He is the most famous of all the Egyptian pharaohs, not for the greatness or length of his reign as he died when he was just a teenager, but because his tomb was discovered intact in 1922 in the Valley of the Kings, complete with a wealth of priceless treasures. We don't know for sure why or how he died, but studies of his mummy have revealed that he had a serious, long-term illness, as well as an infected broken leg.

The gold funerary mask of Tutankhamen was discovered in his tomb.

IDIA OF BENIN, FIRST IYOBA

Idia was a famous figure in Benin history. Following the death of her husband, Oba (King) Ozolu in 1504, she helped to raise and lead an army for her son Esigie to fight his brother Arhuaran. Esigie eventually defeated Arhuaran to become the next Oba. During this civil war, the Igala peoples to the north attempted a rebellion against Benin. Esigie's forces defeated them too. Idia's courage and skill in leading the army helped deliver these victories. To reward her, Oba Esigie created a new position for her called the Iyoba, or queen mother.

An ivory mask of Idia of Benin. It was later looted by British invaders.

NZINGA, FREEDOM FIGHTER

Ana Nzinga became leader of the kingdom of Ndongo, in today's Angola, in 1624. Portuguese slave traders (see page 26) were very powerful at this time in Ndongo, and Ana made alliances to help fight them. Ndongo was declared a free country the following year, meaning that Africans who had become enslaved by the Portuguese could become free if they reached Ndongo. By 1629 Ana's forces and allies had captured the neighbouring state of Matamba. This too was declared a free country. Ana made an alliance with Dutch forces, pitting them against the Portuguese. However, the Portuguese later defeated the Dutch and Ana retreated to the hills of Matamba, where she continued to lead a powerful resistance movement against the Portuguese.

Queen Ana Nzinga of Ndongo and Matamba.

WEST AFRICAN EMPIRES

Three medieval gold-based empires rose and fell in West Africa: ancient Ghana, Mali and Songhai. Ghana led from 300 CE to 1240. Mali dominated from 1240 to 1433, and Songhai was at its strongest from 1469 to 1591.

LAND OF GOLD

Ancient Ghana was a major empire in West Africa. Beginning in 300 CE with the first of its kings, Ghana became an empire by around 700, its wealth growing through trade and by taking tribute from the neighbouring states it had conquered. By the 10th and 11th centuries, it ruled half of West Africa. A 10th century document described the ruler of Ghana as the richest man on Earth, as he controlled its valuable gold mines.

RULED BY GHANA

Medieval Mali was the second major empire in West Africa. It began as a kingdom under ancient Ghanaian rule in 800 CE. However, Mali turned the tables on Ghana, destroying its capital, Kumbi Saleh, in 1240, and taking over its lands.

The ancient Ghana settlement of Chinguetti is now a UNESCO World Heritage Site.

A map showing the empire of Mali and its riches in around 1330. Its ruler, Mansa Musa, is shown sitting on a gold throne.

Djenné's Great Mosque is built from earth bricks.

INDEPENDENT MALI

By the 14th century, Mali had become one of the richest land empires in the world through its control of profitable gold, salt and copper trades. Mansa Musa, who ruled Mali from around 1312, was the greatest of the Malian kings. Historians have estimated the net worth of the 25 richest people in all human history. They ranked Mansa Musa I at number one with a fortune of around US $400 billion!

THE SONGHAI EMPIRE

As Mali grew weaker in the 16th century, Songhai rose to become the next major West African empire, eventually taking over Mali's lands. Its great ruler, Sunni Ali Ber, expanded Songhai's territory and its trading routes, bringing in more wealth. The Songhai cities of Djenné and Timbuktu have preserved heritage from the great days of Mali and Songhai. In the centre of Djenné stands the Great Mosque. Beginning life in the 11th century as a palace, it became a mosque in 1204, as the religion of Islam became increasingly important to the empire.

OLD LITERATURE

Writings from the famous universities of Timbuktu and Djenné still exist today, including law books, business contracts, books on astronomy and algebra, and even poems praising the importance of tea!

A book on astronomy, dating back to the Songhai Empire.

THE NIGERIA REGION

The Nigeria region is rich in cultural heritage, dating back 3,000 years to the ancient art of the civilisation of Nok.

NOK ART

In 1928, tin miners in central Nigeria stumbled upon some terracotta sculptures and figurines of people and animals from an ancient Iron Age civilisation. Iron and stone tools were also discovered near the site. Historians now call this civilisation 'Nok' and date the art from around 1000 BCE to CE 300. Little is known about the Nok people but we know they could work with iron as smelting furnaces have been discovered. It is also believed that they grew and farmed crops.

Nok sculptures have distinctive eyes and often have elaborate hairstyles.

YORUBA

The Yoruba city-states existed from around 600 to the 1800s CE. They introduced yam-farming, cheese-making and horse-breeding to West Africa. They had brilliant metalworkers, weavers, carvers and potters. The cultural capital was the city state of Ile-Ife, but Oyo grew to become the largest state. Through diplomacy, trade and war, it conquered most of the other Yoruba city-states, building an empire that lasted from around the 1600s to the 1820s. It also seized the kingdom of Dahomey to the west.

SLAVE STATE

Dahomey became one of the largest slave trading (see p.26–27) powers in West Africa. It sold other Africans captured as prisoners to buy guns from Europe, with which it hoped to defend itself. It also wanted to free itself from Yoruba rule.

BENIN

The kingdom of Benin rose from around CE 900. Led by a succession of kings known as obas, Benin grew in power and influence after 1440. It traded not only with its African neighbours, but also with Europe, in goods such as ivory, cotton, palm oil and animal skins. Benin's capital, Benin City, boasted a set of huge city walls, which stretched for over 15,000 km – then the largest construction work in the world. By the 1860s though, Benin's power had declined. It was also at risk from Britain, which wanted to take over the region for its rich resources. In 1897, the British invaded Benin and made it part of the British Empire. They set fire to the capital and seized many of Benin's artefacts.

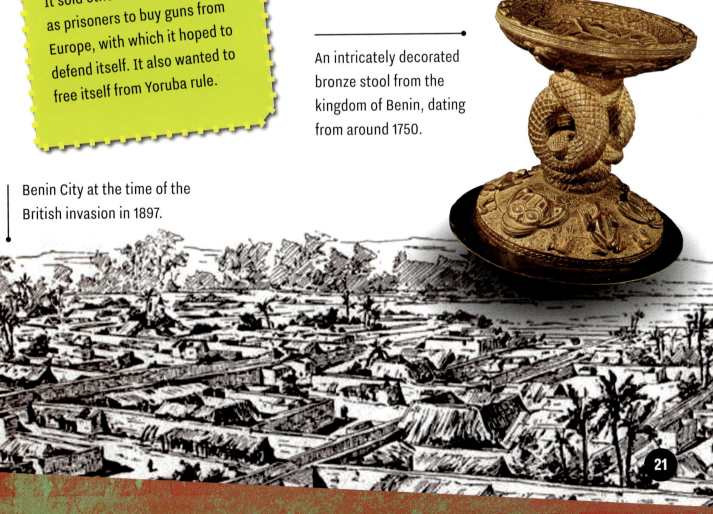

An intricately decorated bronze stool from the kingdom of Benin, dating from around 1750.

Benin City at the time of the British invasion in 1897.

GREAT ZIMBABWE AND MUNHUMUTAPA

In southern Africa, a gold-rich civilisation also flourished in medieval times. Beginning as a city-state in the 11th century, an empire called Munhumutapa prospered from around 1200 to 1629. Hundreds of its mysterious stone courts survive in ruined form today.

STONE SETTLEMENT

Great Zimbabwe was an important settlement in Zimbabwe, dating back to Iron Age times. It consists of 12 groups of stone buildings, spread over around 8 hectares. The world 'Zimbabwe' means stone houses in Shona, the local language. One of the buildings is a mighty hilltop fortress that overlooks the entire area.

An estimated 18,000 people lived in Great Zimbabwe in the 14th century, working in the gold trade, growing crops and keeping cattle. Small thatched homes were once found all over the area, both inside and outside the thick city walls. Eventually though, Great Zimbabwe was abandoned and fell into decline.

FROM KINGDOM TO EMPIRE

The Great Zimbabwe hilltop fortress was built in the 11th century. The rulers of the fortress would go on to become the rulers of a great empire, Munhumutapa, which held power over the whole region. It grew wealthy through trade in gold and other metals, and ivory, and was defended by a well-trained army. The empire dominated the southern Africa region until it was overthrown by the Portuguese in 1629.

A 17th century map of the Munhumutapa Empire.

GOLD TECHNOLOGY

In medieval times, the southern Africans mined an estimated 43 million tons of gold ore. From this, they produced around 700 tons of pure gold. They were also skilled goldsmiths. They made gold ornaments, jewellery and weapons, and plated iron and bronze with thin sheets of beaten gold. Gold thread was even woven into cloth.

Gold is one of Africa's most precious trading goods and made some African kingdoms very wealthy.

The Great Enclosure at Great Zimbabwe may at one time have been home to a local ruler.

IN FOCUS

TREASURES OF AFRICA

The great pyramids of Egypt are famous all over the world. But Africa is also rich in many other historical treasures.

TOWERING TOMB

The Great Pyramid of Giza is one of the most important structures in world history. Ordered to be built by Pharaoh Khufu, the second pharaoh of Dynasty 4, it consists of 2.3 million blocks of shiny limestone and tough granite and is as high as a 40-storey building. The blocks, which weigh between 2.5 and 7 tons, came from Aswan, which was around 800 km away. Historians still do not know how the ancient Egyptians transported the blocks but believe they may have used sledges, rollers and levers to raise the blocks into place. Herodotus (see page 10), wrote that the Great Pyramid took 30 years to build, with 100,000 labourers working in shifts.

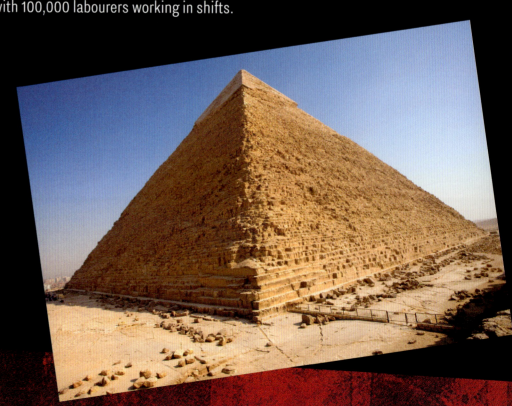

The Great Pyramid of Giza was built in around 2560 BCE. It was the tallest structure in the world for nearly 4,000 years.

An Igbo-Ukwu bronze vase shaped like a shell and decorated with a crouching leopard figure.

ANCIENT ARTEFACTS

Discovered by a farmer digging a well on his land in 1938, a treasure trove of arts and crafts were excavated in the Igbo territories of eastern Nigeria. They were made by a culture known as the Igbo-Ukwu during the 9th and 10th centuries CE, and were believed to form part of a ruler's burial goods. More than 700 artworks were found during the excavations. They were exquisitely cast in bronze, copper and copper-alloy, and included pendants, copper chains, wristlets, ornaments, vessels made to look like seashells, drinking cups, cooking woks, sword scabbards and a copper altar stand. Also found were fly whisks!

'WHITE GOLD' WORKS OF ART

Sapi artisans in Sierra Leone produced elegant works carved from ivory during the 15th and 16th centuries. These were bought by Portuguese traders and sold in Europe, where these pieces became luxury items, exchanged as gifts between the royal courts of Europe. They included finely crafted hunting horns, salt cellars, forks and spoons. Other famous ivory works were made in the empire of Benin (see page 21). Benin and Sapi artists were trained through apprenticeship systems and spent their lives perfecting their craft in the workshops of masters.

An intricate ivory salt cellar lid from Sierra Leone, dating from 1he 15th century.

THE ENSLAVED

From the 15th century, Africa faced the growing threat of slave traders. From small beginnings, the slave trade would plunge Africa into a horror lasting for 400 years. For the people captured and enslaved, they faced lives of brutality and misery.

FIRST RAIDS

In 1441 Portuguese sailors led raids along the West African coast, kidnapping 12 Africans from Morocco. On their return, the sailors offered the captives to Prince Henry of Portugal. This raid would start a dark chapter of history, as powerful European countries, including Portugal, Spain, Britain, the Netherlands and France, saw the potential for a cheap source of workers and enslaved Africa's peoples in greater and greater numbers.

Elmina Castle in Ghana was built by the Portuguese in 1482. Thousands of enslaved Africans were held here before being taken to the Americas.

Enslaved Africans at work at a cotton plantation in the southern USA in the 19th century.

TRADING LIVES FOR GOODS

At first, the African captives were transported to Europe or islands off the coast of Africa. Later, they were transported by ship across the Atlantic to the Americas, to work in the new European colonies there. Here, the enslaved produced foods, such as sugar and rice, and products, such as tobacco, that were shipped on to Europe. From Europe, goods such as cloth, iron products, alcohol and firearms were sold in return to enslavers in Africa.

TERRIBLE JOURNEY

The voyage across the Atlantic to the Americas in overcrowded ships was harsh and dangerous. Often, anyone who appeared ill was simply thrown overboard to stop disease spreading. Around 20 per cent of people did not survive the journey. Those who did were sold on arrival at auctions to the highest bidder.

LIFE FOR THE ENSLAVED

Enslaved Africans worked on sugar, cotton, tobacco and rubber plantations and in diamond and iron ore mines. Others helped build houses or worked as servants in the home. The work was hard and punishing and many enslaved Africans died young. They were also often cruelly treated, as they were viewed as less than human.

HUGE TOLL

It is estimated that between 10 and 12 million Africans were enslaved and transported to the Americas during the slave trade.

RESISTANCE

By the 18th century, global resistance against enslavement and the slave trade was building.

BRITISH ABOLITIONISTS

In Britain, the Society for the Abolition of the Slave Trade was formed in 1787. Members included Ottobah Cugoano and Olaudah Equiano, both of whom had previously been enslaved and were also members of the Sons of Africa, an organisation that worked for total emancipation (freedom) for enslaved Africans. The Society wrote letters and pamphlets and toured Britain, drawing attention to the cruelty of the slave trade and urging people to boycott its products, such as sugar. It influenced people such as the Member of Parliament (MP) William Wilberforce. In 1791, Wilberforce proposed the first bill to abolish slavery, but it was defeated. Wilberforce returned to Parliament with a new bill every year until the Slave Trade Abolition Bill was eventually passed in 1807.

Olaudah Equiano (c.1745–1797) bought his freedom and became a successful writer.

French forces battle Haitian rebels during the Haitian Revolution (see page 29).

THE HAITIAN REVOLUTION

In Haiti, the Africans staged a revolution against their French enslavers, beginning in 1791. Boukman Dutty, an African priest, began the uprising. After Dutty was killed, the former slave Toussaint L'Ouverture continued the fight and secured freedom for Haiti's slaves. He later became ruler of the island, alongside the French. His actions provoked the French leader Napoleon however, and L'Ouverture was captured and imprisoned. It was left to one of his generals, Jean-Jacques Dessalines, to complete the revolution in late 1803. Haiti became an independent country in 1804.

MEXICAN LEADER
Vincente Guerrero, a soldier of African and Native American ancestry, helped Mexico gain its independence from Spain in 1821. He became Mexico's first Black president and abolished slavery in the country in 1829.

JAMAICAN EMANCIPATION

In Jamaica, Sam Sharpe, an educated enslaved man and Baptist preacher, led 60,000 enslaved Africans to demand better pay and more freedom. When this was refused, they destroyed plantations and killed plantation owners in the Baptist War of 1831–1832. Despite being captured and executed, Sharpe's actions forced the hand of the British, who passed laws abolishing the enslavement of Africans in the British colonies in 1838.

Jamaican rebels celebrate the burning of the Roehampton Estate in Jamaica in 1832.

IN FOCUS

AFRICAN RELIGIONS

Africa is home to ancient, diverse religions that have spread around the world. Two of the best-known are those of the Yoruba and the Dogon. Africa, and in particular, Ethiopia, has also nurtured faiths including Judaism, Christianity and Islam.

YORUBA

The Yoruba religion had its origins in the 16 Yoruba kingdoms, now in Nigeria. As Africans were enslaved and deported to other parts of the world, the Yoruba religion spread to the Americas. It formed a large part of the culture of Black people in Cuba, Trinidad and Brazil. In some of these countries, the Yoruba religion has been combined with Christianity. The Yoruba divide the world into Aiya, the Earth and Orun, the sky, where the chief god Oludumare, lives. Followers of Yoruba aim to improve their 'Iwa' or character.

ANCIENT FAITH
The Yoruba religion is believed to be thousands of years old. It is one of the most popular faiths in the world, and is followed by millions of people in Africa and the Americas today.

Followers of the Yoruba faith gather each August in Osogbo in Nigeria to celebrate the river goddess, Oshun.

30

DOGON

The Dogon religion has its origins among the Dogon, a people who lived in the Bandiagara Cliffs of Mali around 3,000 years ago. Followers of Dogon believe in a god called Amma, who created the universe from an egg which, when broken, scattered its contents far and wide, forming the planets and stars. The Dogon also follow animism – the idea that everything on Earth, including trees, animals and rocks, has a soul.

The Dogon are famous for their mask dances which are held to mark rituals and special occasions.

AXUMITE JUDAISM, CHRISTIANITY AND ISLAM

Axum (see page 14) has some of the oldest Judaic, Christian and Islamic history in the world. Coins issued by Emperor Ezana in around 330 CE were the first Christian coins in the world, while two Ethiopian manuscripts called the *Abba Garima Gospels* are thought to be the oldest illustrated Christian manuscripts in the world. Ethiopian Judaism is regarded as the closest form of Judaism to that of ancient times. Ethiopia also has an important history in the evolution of Islam. In around 615 CE, the Prophet (or some say his followers) spent time in Ethiopia under Emperor Armah. Armah also offered sanctuary to some of the first converts to Islam fleeing persecution in Arabia.

Ethiopian Jewish leaders, known as Kessim, prepare for the Sigd holiday in Israel.

COLONIALISM

During the 19th century, Africa was once again under attack, as the European powers used the continent to increase their influence and power. While some rulers resisted, eventually Africa was almost completely under European control.

THE SCRAMBLE FOR AFRICA

Towards the end of the 19th century, with no real chance to recover from the slave trade, Africa faced the threat of colonialism. During a conference in Berlin held in 1884–1885, European nations, including Great Britain, France, Portugal, Belgium and Germany, agreed to divide, or colonise, Africa between them and seize its rich resources for themselves. This became known as the Scramble for Africa.

FIGHTING BACK

Some African rulers led their people to battle to resist being colonised. Among these were the Mahdi in Sudan, Behanzin in Dahomey, Queen Mother Yaa Asantewaa in the Ashanti Empire (Ghana), Lobenguela in Matabeleland (Zimbabwe) and Cetewayo in the Zulu Empire (South Africa). One famous African victory was at Adwa, Ethiopia, in 1896. Led by Emperor Menelik II, the Ethiopian victory over the Italian invaders secured Ethiopian independence for another 40 years. However, the European powers were soon able to use a deadly new invention: the first fully automatic machine gun. This weapon gave the colonisers a huge advantage. Eventually, the European leaders carved up the continent between them.

The cartoon shows the leaders of Europe dividing up Africa like a cake.

Menelik II on horseback at the Battle of Adwa.

TAKING OVER

The Europeans decided what the official languages were going to be in the countries they had colonised, and created the boundaries that African countries have today. Those boundaries bore no resemblance to the ancient African states or kingdoms.

SEGREGATION AND APARTHEID

The colonisers also soon imposed systems to discriminate against the conquered Africans. Africans were not allowed to walk in certain parts of towns unless they had business there as servants. Signs such as 'No Africans allowed' or 'For Europeans only' could be seen all over Africa. An even more extreme version of this was practised in South Africa. Known as apartheid, it divided South Africans by their colour and forced each group to live apart from each other, at work, at home and in schools. Land Acts, passed by the South African government, awarded more than 80 per cent of farmland to whites.

FREE COUNTRIES
By the start of the First World War in 1914, the only remaining independent African countries were Liberia and Ethiopia.

Apartheid-era signs at a train station in South Africa.

INDEPENDENCE FOR AFRICA

Pan Africanists were a group of Africans that called for independence from colonial rule. Beginning with some people of African origin living outside Africa, Pan-Africanism gained support from Africans in Africa itself. It eventually led to countries gaining their freedom, though not without a struggle.

CALLS FOR ACTION

By the early 20th century, nearly all of Africa was under the direct rule of Europe. In 1900 Henry Sylvester Williams, a Trinidadian lawyer, called the first of six Pan-African meetings in London with the aims of ending colonial rule in Africa, and achieving more equality and better rights for Africans and people of African descent.

THE UNIA

In the US, Jamaican activist Marcus Garvey founded the Universal Negro Improvement Association (UNIA) in 1914. He urged Africans everywhere to unite and take pride in their culture and encouraged Black industry, helping to set up factories, printing presses, restaurants and a hotel. Soon, the UNIA had 1,100 branches in more than 40 countries.

Marcus Garvey encouraged Black nationalism.

An invitation to the first Pan-African Conference in July 1900.

TIME FOR CHANGE

By the time of the Fifth Pan-African Congress in England in 1945, many Africans from Africa were in attendance, including three future presidents. For the first time, the Congress called for African independence. At last, change was on the way. Led by Kwame Nkrumah, Ghana's pro-independence CCP party won several key elections, and was granted its independence from Britain in 1957. Other European colonies soon followed. Nigeria became independent in 1960, the Belgian Congo in 1960 and Sierra Leone in 1961.

People celebrate their country's forthcoming independence in the streets of the then Belgian Congo in 1960.

THE SOUTHERN AFRICAN STRUGGLE

However, in southern Africa, Europeans were determined to hold on to their conquered territories and rejected African claims for independence. In Angola and Mozambique, armed movements fought the Portuguese for 14 long, bitter years, finally becoming independent in 1975. In Rhodesia (now Zimbabwe), Africans began a liberation war in 1966 which eventually led to independence in 1980. In Namibia, the pro-independence SWAPO part-defeated the South African regime and declared independence in 1990. Finally, in South Africa, white supremacy rule ended with a landslide victory for the African National Congress in 1994, when Nelson Mandela became the first black president of South Africa. All of Africa was independent at last.

Nelson Mandela fought apartheid for many years before becoming president of South Africa.

IN FOCUS

AFRICAN CULTURE ABROAD

People of African heritage have enriched the culture and given much of value to the rest of the world, from technology to culture and cuisine.

TRADITIONAL TECHNOLOGIES

Enslaved Africans brought their own technologies with them to the Americas, including knowledge of cultivating crops, including bananas, plantains, rice, African yams, ackee, okra, black-eyed peas and watermelons. Africans from the Senegambian region in West Africa were captured and brought to the United States and parts of South America for their knowledge of horsemanship and cattle rearing.

Enslaved Africans at work creating dye from indigo plants at a Caribbean plantation.

Dolly Johnson in the kitchen of the White House, USA.

CUISINE

Enslaved Africans in the Americas created new forms of cuisine out of the rations they were fed on the plantations, and were also influenced by Native American cuisine. They fused these ideas with traditional West African cuisine to create soul food. They ate cornbread, fried catfish and barbecued ribs, and included cooked greens such as collards and beets in their dishes. Soul food became so celebrated that Dolly Johnson, a famous African-American chef, would one day become the head cook for Benjamin Harrison, the 23rd President of the USA.

Feijoada is a rich stew made with pork and black beans and sometimes topped with toasted cassava.

In Brazil, Creole cuisine developed from African origins. Enslaved Africans used traditional ingredients such as cassava, corn and couscous, and flavoured their dishes with coconut and chilli. Feijoada, the national dish of Brazil, was originally created by enslaved Africans.

DANCE

Enslaved African Americans created plantation dances that spread across the world, including the Cakewalk, in which they mocked the formal dances of plantation owners, the Turkey Trot and the Bunny Hug. The Bunny Hug evolved into the ballroom dance known as the Foxtrot. Candombe is a folk dance form that originated in 17th and 18th century Angola and was performed by enslaved Africans in Uruguay. Influenced by the candombe, Black Argentinians in Buenos Aires created the tango, while the rumba is a ballroom dance of Afro-Cuban folk origins. Other famous dances of Black origin include the mambo, the cha-cha-cha and the jive.

Dancers perform the candombe in Montevideo, Uruguay.

AFTER INDEPENDENCE

Despite great optimism at independence, the first years were challenging. Many of the new African nations did not achieve real independence, as colonial powers still controlled the global system of economics. Internally, they faced the wranglings of the different ethnic groups within countries fighting over limited resources.

THE COST OF INDEPENDENCE

Many of Africa's newly independent countries were not prepared for self-rule. Some countries faced bloody civil wars, famines and the seizure of power by the military, known as coups. In many cases, hundreds of thousands of people fled these conflicts and ended up in refugee camps in other countries. Often, foreign interference played a part in these conflicts and ended up prolonging them, as foreign powers assisted one side or the other with their own interests.

A toppled statue of Ghana's ex-leader Kwame Nkrumah. He was overthrown in a coup in 1966.

DICTATORS

African leaders who fought for independence were sometimes removed by corrupt leaders sponsored by the former colonial powers, including the Democratic Republic of the Congo (DRC), the second largest country in Africa. In 1961 army officer Colonel Mobutu seized control of the DRC during a bitter civil war and ruled the country until 1997. Supported by the US and other western powers, Mobutu amassed a huge personal fortune and lived a life of luxury, while most of his people were poor and deprived.

THE COLD WAR
Newly independent Africa was affected by the Cold War (1947–1991) between the USA and the Soviet Union. The Cold War countries supported opposing African regimes and interfered with their politics, leaving an impact still felt today.

President Mobutu shakes hands with the then president of the USA, Ronald Reagan, in 1984.

The BRICS member countries' leaders at a summit in 2023. BRICS stands for Brazil, Russia, India, China and South Africa.

FINDING THEIR IDENTITY

In the years since independence, the many countries of Africa have worked hard to establish ways of government that work for their people, rather than for foreign powers. Many still have strong ties to the European countries that used to colonise them, which can help them to build global partnerships. In 2010, South Africa joined the BRICS bloc, a group of fast-growing economies that work closely together, particularly in trade.

AFRICA TODAY – CHALLENGES

Africa has made huge progress in the 60 years since most of its countries gained independence. However, some of the poverty and inequality that has plagued the continent since the slave trade has remained. Poverty has a chain of negative consequences for African countries.

THE POVERTY CYCLE

Colonial powers often made sure that the newly independent countries did not inherit an economic infrastructure. Poor people everywhere have the least resources to create businesses. Fewer businesses mean high levels of unemployment. High unemployment means fewer people can afford to feed, clothe, and house their families, and pay tax to the government. Consequently, governments have little money to build roads, schools and hospitals, and so the cycle continues.

Children learning English at a village school in Malawi. Schools in Africa often lack adequate facilities, from computers and sports facilities to sanitation.

MIGRATION

Poverty is a leading cause of Africa's high migration rates. Africa's young adults are most likely to want to migrate and most move within the continent to look for work. Outside Africa, the most popular destinations are Europe and North America. Another reason for migration is fleeing political violence and repression. Some African governments are undemocratic and ordinary people have little political power. In some countries, human rights are limited. Migrants often undertake dangerous journeys to reach new lands, while the countries they leave behind lose valuable workers. The countries that take in migrants can struggle with overcrowding and their essential resources, such as water, can be strained.

CLIMATE CHANGE

One of the biggest challenges facing Africa is climate change. Although Africa contributes far less to global greenhouse emissions than more developed regions, it is warming up to two times faster than the rest of the world. This has disastrous effects on growing crops and the supply of fresh water, which will in turn make it harder to ensure Africans have enough to eat and drink. Climate change is also leading to greater desertification, putting more pressure on Africa's precious farmland.

Migrants from North Africa arrive at the port of Taranto in Italy.

ON THE MOVE

In 2020, the African countries that hosted the most migrants were South Africa, the Ivory Coast and Uganda. Nigeria was also a popular destination. People are attracted to these countries for work, education and other life opportunities.

Climate change is causing more and longer droughts. This reservoir in South Africa has run dry.

AFRICA TODAY – SUCCESSES

Africa today is looking to the future. As the world becomes more globally linked, Africa is building new relationships and partnerships, both inside and outside the continent, while retaining its own identity.

TRADING TOGETHER

During the colonial period, African countries did most of their business with Europe. Huge taxes were charged on goods sold from one African country to another. However, this began to change in 2018 with the creation of the African Continental Free Trade Area. This allows the buying and selling of goods between member countries without taxes having to be paid. The Free Trade Area came into operation in 2021 as the largest free trade zone in the world. It links 54 countries and 1.3 billion people together. This is expected to create more incomes in African countries and lift 30 million people out of extreme poverty. The creation of free trade across Africa is part of a series of initiatives that the African Union, created in 2002, has planned as part of its vision to empower Africa.

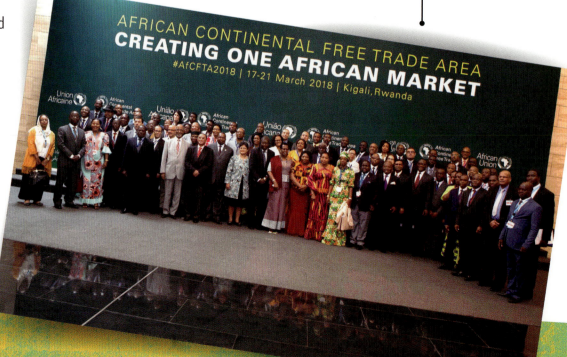

Representatives of member countries celebrate the agreement to create the African Continental Free Trade Area in 2018.

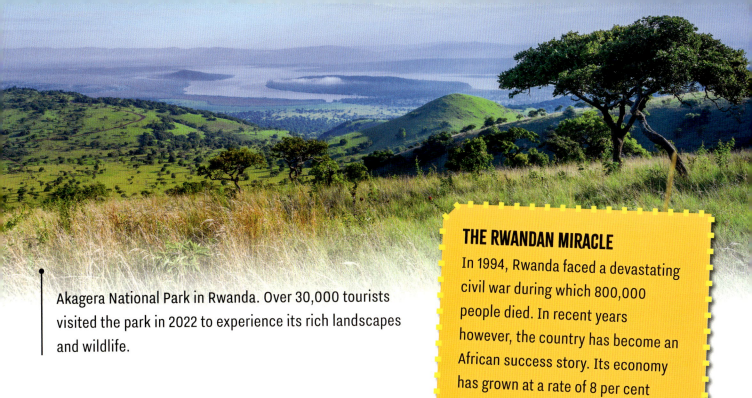

Akagera National Park in Rwanda. Over 30,000 tourists visited the park in 2022 to experience its rich landscapes and wildlife.

IMPROVING HEALTHCARE

Since independence, many African countries have made strides to develop the quality of their healthcare. In the late 1980s, many African countries faced outbreaks of HIV and AIDS. The health professionals in these countries learned many skills from treating these outbreaks. The Covid-19 pandemic was expected by many to devastate Africa. Excluding South Africa, this did not happen. In 2022, the World Health Organization reported the average age expectancy in 47 African countries had increased by ten years since 2000 – a huge achievement.

OPEN TO THE WORLD

African culture is becoming more globally celebrated. People of African heritage today are world leaders, scientists and engineers, sporting superstars, actors and musicians, bringing Africa onto the world stage. It has hosted top sporting events, including the 2010 FIFA Football World Cup. As the 21st century goes on, Africa will continue to grow and develop, fulfilling the promise of its long, rich history.

THE RWANDAN MIRACLE

In 1994, Rwanda faced a devastating civil war during which 800,000 people died. In recent years however, the country has become an African success story. Its economy has grown at a rate of 8 per cent per year since 2001, while the percentage of its population living in poverty fell from 57 per cent in 2006 to 39 per cent in 2017. Rwanda has also made strides towards gender equality. Over 63 per cent of its members of parliament are now women. The world average is just 22 per cent.

South Africa fans celebrate the start of the FIFA World Cup in 2010. The tournament was praised for raising the profile of African sport.

TEACHING AFRICAN HISTORY

The teaching of African history can be easily integrated into history lessons and not just restricted to lessons during Black History Month. There are also valuable online resources and museum collections to visit.

At Key Stage One, the National Curriculum advises that children should be taught:

- 'Changes within living memory'. The content that fits this criterion is very broad. Teachers keen to include black content could give the simple example of buying food. At one time, foods aimed at African and Caribbean people in Britain were only available from market stalls or specialised African Caribbean shops. Now, mainstream supermarkets sell these widely.

At Key Stage Two, the National Curriculum advises that children should be taught about:

- 'The achievements of the earliest civilisations e.g. Ancient Egypt'. In this book, we have dedicated pages to show the achievements of ancient Egypt placed within its correct African context.
- 'A non-European society that provides contrasts with British history such as Benin (West Africa) c. 900–1300 CE.' This offers another opportunity to include early African history into the mainstream teaching of school history.

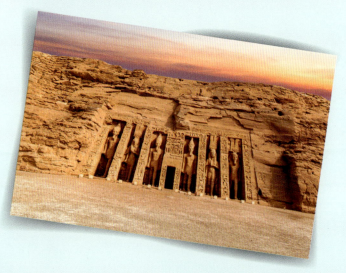

At Key Stage Three, the National Curriculum advises that pupils should be taught:
• 'Britain's transatlantic slave trade: its effects and its eventual abolition.' This book includes much of this content.

ONLINE RESOURCES

Some good resources for Key Stage Two history teaching on the Kingdom of Benin are listed below. For ancient Egypt, there are just too many resources to list here!

https://www.ks2history.com/benin-guide
https://www.bbc.co.uk/bitesize/topics/zpvckqt
https://digitalbenin.org/

The Black Secret Education Programme at (www.theblacksecret.co.uk) is a resource for teachers and parents to get up to speed with African history. This programme helps adults master the information so that they can confidently teach this information.

MUSEUM COLLECTIONS

The museums in England very often do not have enough African artefacts from any one civilisation to justify a whole school trip. However, the best museum collection in Britain for African history is the British Museum and contains excellent collections from Ancient Egypt, Sudan and Benin. The Petrie Museum of Egyptian Archaeology in London is a good resource for ancient Egyptian history. The World Museum in Liverpool also has an excellent collection of African artefacts. Liverpool also has the International Slavery Museum which is highly recommended.

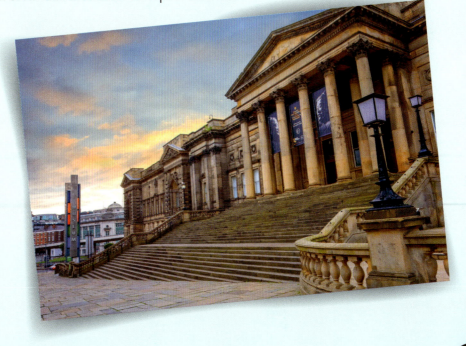

TIMELINE

PRE-HISTORY

6.5 million years ago: The human story begins in Africa, where the first apes to walk upright evolve in East and South Africa.

200,000 years ago: The first modern humans, Homo sapiens, evolve in Africa.

100,000 years ago: Modern humans (Homo sapiens) start to move out of Africa and settle in other parts of the world.

DATES BCE (BEFORE COMMON ERA – YEARS BEFORE 1 BCE/ CE 1)

c.3400: Birth of kingship in the Nubian kingdom of Ta-Seti.
3100–2181: Old Kingdom Period of ancient Egyptian history.
2555–2539: The Great Pyramid at Giza is built.
2040–1786: Middle Kingdom Period of ancient Egyptian history.
2000: Evidence for people smelting iron in the area of modern Nigeria.
1560–1080: New Kingdom Period of ancient Egyptian history.
1322: Death of Pharaoh Tutankhamen.
663: The Assyrians conquer Egypt.
525: The Persians conquer Egypt.
332: The Greeks, led by Alexander the Great, conquer Egypt.
c.100: Axum becomes a great trading city.
30: The forces of Cleopatra VII are defeated by the army of the Roman Empire.
1 BCE/CE 1: Birth of Jesus Christ.

DATES CE (YEARS AFTER COMMON ERA 1 BCE/CE 1)

c.300: Ancient Ghana becomes a kingdom.
330: Christianity becames the state religion of Ethiopia.
639: Arabians invade and occupy Egypt. They conquer all of North Africa by 708.
c.700: The kingdom of ancient Ghana becomes an empire.
c.850: The Igbo-Ukwu culture flourishes in eastern Nigeria.
c.1085: People begin to build Great Zimbabwe, the capital of the Munhumutapa Empire.
1180: Emperor Lalibela begins the construction of the underground churches in Lalibela in Ethiopia.
1240–1433: Kingdom of Mali at its greatest.
1375–1591: The Songhai Empire is at its height.
1441: The Portuguese begin to raid Africa and enslave Africans. This becomes the Transatlantic Slave Trade that lasts for over 400 years.
1787: The Society for the Abolition of the Slave Trade forms in Great Britain. Some US states abolish slavery.
1791: Enslaved Africans in Haiti revolt against the French. Eventually they gain freedom.
1807: The Slave Trade Abolition Act is passed in the British Houses of Parliament.
1831–1832: Sam Sharpe leads the Emancipation War in Jamaica against the British.
1838: Britain finally abolishes the mass enslavement of Africans.
1861–1865: American Civil War. Slavery is abolished in the USA.
1884–1885: European powers at the Berlin Conference agree a plan to seize control of all Africa.
1897: The British army invades Benin.
1900: Henry Sylvester Williams leads the first Pan-African Conference in London.
1945: The Fifth Pan-African Congress calls for independence for Africa.
1948: Apartheid is established across South Africa.
1957: Dr Nkrumah becomes first president of an independent Ghana.
Most African countries gain independence within the next few years.
1974: Angola and Mozambique defeat Portuguese colonialism and win independence.
1994: Nelson Mandela becomes president of South Africa.
2018: The African Continental Free Trade Area is created.

NOTE: Most Egyptologists accept the dates shown in this timeline but some dispute them, citing archaeological evidence that indicates moving the dates back in time by about 2,000 years or more. So the Old Kingdom Period dates would be 5660–4188 BCE; Middle Kingdom Period 3448–3182 BCE and New Kingdom Period 1709–1095 BCE. The earliest dates are often very unsecure whichever dating system you follow, as dates are only certain after 664 BCE.

GLOSSARY

Abolition The formal ending of the slave trade.

Activist Someone who works to bring about social or political change.

Apartheid The system of government in South Africa that kept white and non-white people apart.

Archaeologist Someone who studies the past by looking at the remains of old buildings and objects.

Artefact Any object made by humans.

City-state An area made up of a city and the land around it, which it controls.

Civil war A war within a country or state.

Civilisation An organised human society, with its own structure and culture.

Cold War The period of tension, following the end of the Second World War, between the Soviet Union and the USA and each side's allies.

Colonialism When more powerful countries or states take over less powerful ones to increase their own territory and seize the colony's resources.

Colony A country or land controlled by a more powerful country.

Conquer Take over a place by force.

Discriminate To treat a person or group of people better or worse than others.

Dynasty A line of rulers belonging to the same family.

Empire A group of nations or territories under the control of a single ruler.

Enslave To make someone a slave.

Indigenous Belonging to a place.

Iron Age The period of time in history when people began to work with iron.

Medieval The time in history between around the 5th and 15th centuries CE.

Manuscript An old piece of writing.

Migrate To move, often to find work.

Nubia The land immediately south of the ancient Egyptian border. It includes the civilisations in this region, such as Ta-Seti and Kush.

Obelisk A tall stone pillar, built to commemorate a person or event.

Ore Rock or earth with traces of metal in them.

Plantation A large area of land where crops such as tobacco, sugar and cotton are grown.

Prehistory The time in history before anything was written down.

Stele An upright stone slab or pillar with writing carved into it.

Tomb A burial place.

White supremacy The belief that white people are superior to all other people.

INDEX

Africa
    landscape 4
    map 4
    migrations 4–5, 41
    (see entries for separate countries)
African Continental Free Trade Area 42
African Union 42
Alexander the Great 11
Americas, the (North/Central/South America) 26–27, 30, 36–37
Ana Nzinga of Ndongo 17
Angola 4, 17, 35, 37

Benin 17, 21, 25, 32
Brazil 30, 37
Britain 5, 15, 17, 21, 26, 28–29, 32, 34–35
    abolitionists 28–29

challenges of independence 40–41
Christianity 11, 13–15, 30–31
Cleopatra VII 11
climate change 41
colonialism 32–33, 42
    countries gain independence 4, 29, 34–35, 38–39
    post-independence upheaval 38–39
Cugoano, Ottabah 28
cuisines, African influence on 36–37

Dahomey 21, 32
dance, African influence on 37

Democratic Republic of the Congo 4, 39
Dessalines, Jean-Jacques 29
Dutty, Boukman 29

Egypt, ancient 4, 7–14, 24
    Great Pyramid of Giza 24
    Great Sphinx 8
    pharaohs 7–9, 11, 16, 24
    pyramids 8, 24
    temples 8–9
Equiano, Olaudah 28
Eritrea 4, 14
Eswatini 4, 6–7
Ethiopia 4–5, 14–15, 30–33
    Axum 14–15, 31
    churches of Lalibela 15
    Gondar 14–15

France 26, 28–29, 32

Garvey, Marcus 34
Ghana 4, 18, 26, 32, 35, 38
gold 12, 14, 18–19, 22–23
Great Zimbabwe 22–23
Greeks, ancient 4, 10–11, 14, 24

Haiti 28–29
healthcare 43
Herodotus 10, 24
humans, early 5–7
    Cheddar Man 5
    mining 6

Idia of Benin 17
Islam 19, 30–31
Italy 14, 32, 41
Ivory Coast 4, 41

Jamaica 29
Judaism 30–31

Kenya 4, 7
King Taharqo 12–13
Kush 12–13

L'Ouverture, Toussaint 29

Mali 4, 18–19, 31
    Dogon religion 31
Mandela, Nelson 35
Mansa Musa I 18–19
Mobutu, President 39
Morocco 4, 26
Mozambique 35
Munhumutapa 22–23
    Great Zimbabwe 22–23

Namibia 4, 35, 39
Nigeria 4, 20–21, 25, 35, 41
Benin 21, 25 *see also separate Benin entry*
    Igbo-Ukwu 25
    Nok people 20
    Yoruba 21, 30
Nkrumah, Kwame 35, 38
Nubia 7
    pharaohs 7

Pan-African movement 34–35
Persia/Persians 10–11, 14
Portugal 17, 23, 25–26, 32, 35
    slave trade 17, 26
poverty cycle 40–41

Romans, ancient 4, 11, 14
Rwanda 4, 43

Scramble for Africa 32–33
segregation 33
Sharpe, Sam 29
Sierra Leone 4, 25, 35
Sapi 25
slave trade/slavery 17, 21, 24–29, 32, 36–37
Society for the Abolition of the Slave Trade 28
Songhai 18–19
South Africa 4–5, 7, 32, 35, 41, 43
    apartheid 33, 35
Spain 13, 26, 29
Sudan 4, 7, 12–13, 32
    Kush 12–13

Ta-Seti 6–7
transatlantic slave trade 26–29, 32, 40
    abolishing slavery 28–29
Tutankhamen 16

Uganda 4, 41
UNIA (Universal Negro Improvement Association) 34
USA 26–27, 34, 36, 39

Wilberforce, William 28

Zimbabwe 4, 22–23, 32, 35